# a short history of

# ~portland~

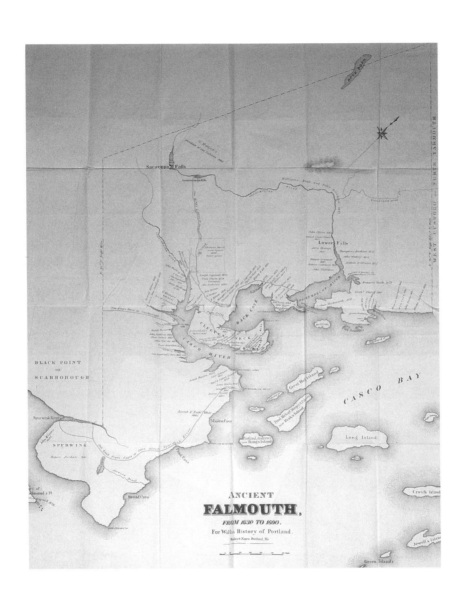

ANCIENT
**FALMOUTH,**
*FROM 1630 TO 1690.*
For Willis History of Portland.

# a short history of

# portland

*Allan Levinsky*

COMMONWEALTH EDITIONS
BEVERLY, MASSSACHUSETTS

*For Vaughn G. Levinsky*

Library of Congress Cataloging-in-Publication Data
Levinsky, Allan M.
  A short history of Portland / Allan M. Levinsky
  p. cm.
Includes bibliographical references and index.
ISBN 978-1-933212-43-2 (alk. paper)
1. Portland (Me.)—History. 2. Portland (Me.)—
  Biography. I. Title
F29.P9L48 2007
974.1'91—dc22    2007044962

Cover images are from the Collections of the
Maine Historical Society

Series design by Laura McFadden Design, Inc.

Printed in the United States of America

Published by Commonwealth Editions
an imprint of Memoirs Unlimited, Inc.
266 Cabot Street, Beverly, MA 01915
www.commonwealtheditions.com

# contents

# from the top of the hill

Often I think of the beautiful town
That is seated by the sea;
Often in thought go up and down
The pleasant streets of that dear old town,
And my youth comes back to me.

—*Henry Wadsworth Longfellow, "My Lost Youth"*

THESE WORDS, WRITTEN BY PORTLAND'S OWN world-famous poet, Henry Wadsworth Longfellow, reflect the sentiment of many who visit this small, very cosmopolitan city. Few realize the highs and lows of its recorded history, which stretches back to the beginnings of the seventeenth century.

Portland rests largely on a three-mile-long peninsula; its sheltered harbor, Casco Bay, and Back Cove surround it on three sides. It is shaped like a giant saddle with hills at both ends. At the eastern end rises Munjoy Hill, with its magnificent view of Casco Bay. At the highest point on the hill sits a tall, red maritime signal tower, now called the Portland Observatory, the last remaining signal tower in the United States. Climbing the 103 steps to its observation cupola, you can look back through time and see the city's history unfold before your eyes.

You can envision the encampments of the Indian tribes on the islands in the bay as they watch with questioning eyes the large sailing ships of the very

Portland Observatory, at the peak of Munjoy Hill, was built by Captain Lemuel Moody in 1807 as a commercial maritime signal tower to notify shipowners of the imminent arrival of their vessels. It stands today as the last remaining signal tower in the country.

early explorers silently, slowly making their way past them as they seek commercial opportunities. Looking west to the bottom of the hill you see the spot where the founders built their first small cabins as they sought a new life in a new place. A short distance from there stood a fort built to protect later colonists from the hostile actions of the French and Indians as they sought to dominate this part of what was then still Massachusetts.

Moving ahead to the eighteenth century, more destruction occurs as a British fleet anchors in the harbor and tries to teach rebellious colonists a lesson by destroying the town with a rain of hot lead. And in the middle of the nineteenth century the destruction continues as the largest fire in the country until then nearly destroys the city.

Through all this, Portland has always managed to raise itself from the ashes and reinvent itself as a better place to live and work. The phoenix is its symbol and *Resurgam*, "I shall rise again," its motto, and its exciting history is a lesson well worth learning as a guide to what makes a great place an even better place. ⌐

# 1
## settlement and uncertainty

FIVE HUNDRED YEARS after Leif Eriksson the Norseman explored the New England coast, and possibly Maine, the French king Francis I sent Giovanni da Verazanno to make an extended examination of Maine shores in 1524. He called it the "Land of the Bad People," probably after seeing hostile eyes peering at him from the shore. Over the next seventy-five years England and France sent others to explore the coast and interior.

The colony of Jamestown, founded in 1607, started exploration of its own and in 1610 began sending fishing vessels to the Gulf of Maine. The earliest movement for settlement of the area, however, did not begin until Captain John Smith visited the Maine coast in 1614 and after returning to England wrote his *Description of New England,* which encouraged Englishmen to settle in Maine. He named the present Casco Bay "Harrington's Bay," and what is now Portland he called "Dartmouth."

The native population had occupied the Casco Bay area for thousands of years, living off the abundance of food from both land and sea. The sea provided them with clams, fish, and duck, while deer and other game roamed the woods. They supplemented this with crops of corn, beans, and squash. Finally, the Europeans made their way to this bountiful place, which the Indians called Machegonne.

In 1621 King James I issued a charter to a group of noblemen who had formed the Council for New England, granting them most of the land that is now Maine. They, in turn, in 1622 granted to the man considered the most important in the settling of Maine, Sir Fernando Gorges, and his partner, Captain John Mason, the land now comprising New Hampshire and Maine. The two men divided the territory between them, and Gorges received what is now Maine. The following year, 1623, Christopher Levett was granted six thousand acres and, accompanied by a small group of men, settled on an island in Casco Bay, probably the present House Island. He got along well with the Natives in the area and their chief, Skitterygusset. After building a stockade and naming his territory York, he remained only a short time before returning to England to recruit others to come back with him. Unfortunately, England was then at war with Spain, and Levett was ordered to take command of one of the king's ships. He died in 1630; the crew he had left on House Island deserted, and the settlement was never heard from again.

In 1628 a trader named Walter Bagnall arrived on nearby Richmond Island, off Cape Elizabeth, where he set up a trading post and immediately began cheating the Indians. Finally, three years later, in 1631, their patience worn thin, the Indians got even by murdering Bagnall.

By 1630 the English had set up small communities from midcoast Pemaquid to Kittery in the far south, and land grants were generously and quickly passed out, which caused much contentiousness among the grantees. One such dispute led to the settlement of the Portland peninsula, also called Falmouth Neck, or the Neck.

Among the fortune seekers who came and helped themselves to whatever land they could find was George Cleeve, a native of Plymouth,

# George Cleeve

OCCUPATION: Farmer, land speculator

LIFETIME: ?–1666

FAMILY: Born in Plymouth, England. Wife, Joan; daughter, Elizabeth.

ACCOMPLISHMENTS: First settler on Portland Peninsula in 1632. Began farming and lumbering and expanded into land speculation. His importance grew as he acquired large land holdings and greater influence. Cleeve was responsible for bringing more settlers into what was then called Falmouth Neck. He became a judge, the head of Maine's colonial Supreme Court, and president of the province. His final years were marked by poverty and illness.

GREATEST CONTROVERSY: Cleeve's life on the peninsula was a turbulent one and much of it was spent either suing or being sued by his chief rival, John Winter. Acting as his own lawyer, he took advantage of every aspect of the law in his favor but was not above bending the law to his own advantage.

George Cleeve

England. He settled on Richmond Island with his wife, Joan, and daughter, Elizabeth. Along with a partner, Richard Tucker, who had settled on the island earlier, he established a prosperous farming and trading business. They were there only two years before a man named John Winter arrived suddenly in 1632 carrying formal documents issued by the Council of

Plymouth under the authority of King Charles. He represented Robert Trelawney and Moses Goodyear, who had been granted a tract of land that included the area occupied by George Cleeve.

Cleeve and Tucker were ordered to leave immediately unless they were willing to become rent-paying tenants, something their independent nature would not allow. Instead, they left everything, loaded their boat with Cleeve's family, his servant, and their personal belongings, and sailed toward Casco Bay and the peninsula. They found a suitable spot at the present Fore and Hancock Streets, next to a stream of pure water, and became the first white settlers of Portland.

The peninsula was a place of both beauty and utility, and the two men chose land overlooking the harbor to build their cabins on, planting a cornfield and garden next to them. There were now five people living on the Neck, Cleeve, his wife and daughter, Richard Tucker, and Cleeve's black servant, Oliver Weeks. Many years later Weeks would become a person of controversy when descendants of Cleeve attempted to donate a statue of the founding father to the City of Portland. The City politely refused, claiming that Weeks had been a slave, something that has never been proved. It is just as likely that he had been a free indentured servant. Cleeve's statue now stands on private property next to the harbor, very close to the spot he first settled. Richard Tucker acted as the business manager of the new enterprise and carried on the trading and farming; Cleeve managed the land speculations and played a major role by returning to England to secure titles to his land and in general open the way for others to settle here.

Cleeve's life on the Neck was a turbulent one, especially when it came to his relations with John Winter, who had kicked him off Richmond Island, and much of his life was spent either suing or being sued. He usually acted as his own lawyer, the major portion of the litigation consisting of claims and counterclaims by or against John Winter and his son-in-law.

In 1636 Cleeve returned to England to formally secure his property on the Neck. He went to Fernando Gorges and for one hundred pounds sterling received a two-thousand-year lease. Mission accomplished, he returned to the Neck accompanied by a man named Michael Mitton, who would later marry his daughter, Elizabeth. The newlyweds settled on an island within sight of the town. It became known as Mitton's Island and is now called Peaks Island.

For about five years it never occurred to anyone that the small Cleeve settlement was within Trelawny's Cape Elizabeth boundaries. As his busi-

A monument honoring Portland's founder, George Cleeve, and his partner, Richard Tucker, stands on the Eastern Promenade at the foot of Congress Street.

ness enterprises grew, Trelawny realized that he needed more land, and the natural advantages of the harbor at the Neck came to mind. So he claimed Cleeve's land was within his jurisdiction and attempted to take possession, abruptly ordering Cleeve to leave his home. Cleeve resisted and by then had gained a following large enough to make it impractical for Trelawny's agent, John Winter, to enforce his claim and the eviction order. Gorges supported Cleeve's claim, and in 1640 a court was set up at Saco, Maine, and suit was brought against Winter. Cleeve won the suit and was awarded compensation for his initial forced move from Richmond Island, and the title to his land on the Neck was also confirmed by the court. The insistent and arrogant Winter declaring the evidence to be insufficient, disregarded the verdict, and continued his hostilities against Cleeve.

In 1659 George Cleeve sold his homestead and all his land to John Phillips of Boston. The deed was executed by his wife, Joan, and approved by Richard Tucker on August 15, 1660. Phillips permitted Cleeve and his wife to live on a portion of the property and improve the cornfield and the house. The rest of the property was occupied by Phillips's son-in-law George Munjoy, who had moved to the Neck from Boston. He built a house a short distance east of Cleeve's residence. It would remain his home until the destruction of the settlement in 1676.

The name Falmouth was established in 1658 under Massachusetts authority and included what is now Portland, Deering, Cape Elizabeth, South Portland, Westbrook, Falmouth, and the surrounding islands.

Meanwhile, the political situation in England kept changing, causing Cleeve's fortunes to fluctuate. By 1663 his mounting debts finally forced one of his creditors, Robert Jordan, to obtain a warrant attaching his personal property. Cleeve and his wife were roughly treated and evicted from their house. His final years were marked by poverty and illness. His last court appearance was in 1666, and he probably died shortly after that, a very old man with a wife aged nearly ninety-one years.

During his lifetime, George Cleeve was undoubtedly a man of great activity and enterprise. He was a partisan and leader who had to deal with difficulties inconceivable to those of us living in today's world. He is probably buried in Portland's oldest cemetery, Eastern Cemetery, at the corner of Mountfort and Congress Streets. There are many unmarked graves there, and a large portion of the cemetery at the back end is now gone, earth and graves dug up and used as landfill in other parts of the city. There have been no burials there since the nineteenth century. In 1974 it was named to the National Register of Historic Places.

Another distinguished resident of Falmouth Neck was the aforementioned George Munjoy. Married to the daughter of John Phillips, who had purchased Cleeve's land in 1659, he became a large landowner himself, ultimately owning most of what is now Munjoy Hill. Although never a permanent resident, he had first visited the Neck in 1657, finally staying two years later, encouraged by the prospects offered by fishing, agriculture, and trade. A man of education and enterprise, he had sufficient capital to exercise extreme influence on the Neck. In 1659 he built the first jail in Falmouth and in 1665 he went into business after being granted a license by the court to retail wine and liquor. He built a tavern and a house on the beach at the lower end of town, at the foot of Mountfort Street. His house was reinforced and used as a garrison for protection in times of danger. Munjoy bought a four-hundred-acre farm from Thomas Brackett in January 1671, and he also purchased House Island in the harbor. He died in Boston in 1680 at the age of fifty-four.

The area owes much of its prosperity to its calm, protected harbor and the surrounding rivers. One of the more important areas of trade was due to its accessibility and the British navy. In 1652 regular cargoes of masts, cut in the Casco Bay area, were beginning to be shipped to the Royal Navy. Before then masts were shipped only sporadically, and trees were cut from many Maine woodlands. It was when the business became profitable that a stream of settlers from other provinces began to make their way into southern Maine to get their own share of the mast profits. Cutters were paid as much as one hundred pounds a tree, a considerable amount back then.

The trade grew rapidly and finally reached a point where the British

*Henry Mowatt*

OCCUPATION: Career British naval officer

LIFETIME: ?–1798

ACCOMPLISHMENTS: One of Portland's and Maine's greatest foes during the Revolution. Captured while trying to protect a Tory merchant in Falmouth (Portland) in 1775 and released after several days, he returned six months later with a small flotilla under orders to punish certain towns for their open rebellion against the British Crown. An all-day bombardment destroyed Falmouth's shipping and two-thirds of the town. For this action he was advanced in rank and given a formal reception by King George III.

Henry Mowatt

*"... which leads me to feel, not a little, the woes of the innocent of them in particular on the present occasion, from my having it in orders to execute a just punishment on the town of Falmouth, in the name of which authority I previously warn you to remove without delay, the human specie out of the said town, for which purpose I give you the time of two hours."*

needed more control, so they appointed a surveyor of pine to supervise the operation. Only certain trees were used: they had to be white pine, at least twenty-four inches in diameter. These trees were marked with three broad strokes of an axe, which were called the king's broad arrow. Trees with this mark were for the king's use only, but often settlers and farmers needing lumber ignored the mark and cut the trees down anyway, especially when it came time to clear land for crops and houses. By 1729 the British had begun

# Samuel Deane

OCCUPATION: Clergyman, diarist

LIFETIME: 1733–1814

FAMILY: Son of Samuel Deane and Rachel Dwight. Married forty-six years to Eunice Pearson. No children.

ACCOMPLISHMENTS: Graduated from Harvard in 1760 and appointed tutor there five years later. Appointed copastor of the First Parish Church in Portland when dissatisfaction with the Reverend Thomas Smith arose and the affairs of the parish became very depressed. Built a house on Congress Street but was forced to move to Gorham when the British destroyed the town in 1775, though he returned often to preach. His greatest contribution to Portland history lies in his diary, which he kept for fifty-three years, from 1761 until his death in 1814, and in which he described daily life in the town.

Samuel Deane

*"Death has lost all its terrors; I am going to my friend Jesus, for I have seen him this night."*

to enforce the Broad Arrow Act, and anyone caught illegally cutting down the king's trees was fined a hefty one hundred pounds.

Finally, the mast trade grew so large that someone was needed to take charge, and a mast agent was named. The first agent appointed in Falmouth was Colonel Thomas Westbrook, an intelligent and able businessman. He built a lumber camp in Scarborough, hired a large crew, and acquired enough oxen to haul the masts to the river, where they were loaded onto ships and sent to England. The city of Westbrook is named after him.

He was replaced as mast agent by George Tate, who moved to Falmouth from England in 1751. Purchasing a large plot of land next to the Fore River, a convenient spot from which to load masts, he built a big house overlooking the river that still stands today, a popular tourist attraction. The mast trade was over by the Revolution. By then colonists were moving the masts to convenient hiding places to keep them out of British hands.

At the beginning of 1675, Falmouth was a prosperous place with a growing population. More businesses were being established, including mills. This prosperity and growth, however, was, without warning, soon to come to a sudden halt that affected not only Falmouth but all of New England.

For more than a generation relations with the Indians had been friendly. The tribes were happy that the white intruders would trade valuable objects such as knives, hatchets, utensils, and especially shiny beads and blankets for what they considered the less valuable furs and other items. Gradually, however, the differences between the two races were becoming evident, and a feeling of hostility began to develop that would turn out to be uncompromising and deadly. When it became apparent that the strangers from abroad were coming in ever-growing numbers, taking more and more of their land and killing the game they depended on for their subsistence, the Indians decided to put a stop to it. In June 1675 King Philip's War began in Plymouth Colony and quickly spread to Maine.

Metacomet of Pokanoket, known as King Philip, was the leader of Indian forces in the 1670s in what is called King Philip's War. The fighting resulted in great damage and loss of life in New England, including the Province of Maine.

At the beginning of September about twenty Indians attacked the house of a Brunswick, Maine, resident, taking liquor, ammunition, and other things. None of the inhabitants was injured. Soon after that attack, a group of twenty-five Englishmen went to the southern end of Casco Bay to gather corn. They discovered three Indians near some houses a short distance from the water. The party attacked, killing one Indian and wounding another. The third Indian managed to escape and with some nearby friends attacked the Englishmen, wounding several and driving the rest back to their boat and escape. This was the first blood shed in the area, but much more would flow in the months to come.

Many attempts were made to recruit and train able-bodied men into fighting units, but the population was so widely scattered that efforts were useless, and there was little protection against the Indians.

About a week after the incident between the Indians and the corn-gathering Englishmen, the first act of Indian revenge took place in Falmouth against the family of Thomas Wakely. All but one of the eight family members, including a pregnant wife and four children, were killed. Only an eleven-year-old girl survived and was taken prisoner.

At the beginning of 1675 forty widely scattered families lived in town. After the war broke out and the Wakely family was slaughtered, many of the residents scattered to more secure sections of the countryside. This reduced the number of casualties, but the Indians were still able to find enough settlers to vent their anger on.

In August 1676 Falmouth again came under attack, and thirty-four persons were either killed or taken captive. The following month, a number of residents who had been driven from the town made their way to House Island in Casco Bay, only to be killed there by the Indians. The government of Massachusetts sent a militia group to help the residents of Falmouth, but the Indians, learning of the coming of this militia group, managed to avoid them. After a large group attacked Black Point and Richmond Island, hostilities ceased with the coming of a particularly severe winter that deprived the Indians of much-needed ammunition and supplies from their French allies in Canada.

King Philip's War resumed with the arrival of summer, but by November 1677 the Indians seemed to be ready for peace and offered to enter into a treaty. Many tribal members were reluctant to comply and evaded most of the articles. By the summer of 1678 the two groups finally reached agreement and the articles of peace were signed on April 12. The residents were permitted to return to their homes and the captives freed, and thus ended the relentless war that had taken so many lives.

In 1680 an attempt was made by the Massachusetts government to provide some safety to Falmouth's residents with the building of Fort Loyall, designed to provide a place of refuge for the citizens in case of attack. The town was a collection of scattered houses near the fort that stood at the foot

# Samuel Freeman

OCCUPATION: Jurist

LIFETIME: 1743–1831

FAMILY: Eldest son of Enoch Freeman. Married twice, children by both wives.

ACCOMPLISHMENTS: An active Patriot during the Revolutionary War and a member of the provincial congress in 1775. Served in the Massachusetts House of Representatives in 1776 and 1778. Appointed clerk of the county courts in 1775, a position he held for forty-six years, and judge of probate in 1804. Freeman was well thought of by his fellow citizens, and he served them in many other positions of responsibility, including postmaster, town selectman, deacon of the First Parish, president of the Maine Bank, and president of the overseers of Bowdoin College. He was the first to edit the journals of the Reverend Thomas Smith.

Samuel Freeman

of Broad Street, now India Street. The ferry left from the town landing at the foot of Hancock Street, and opposite the town landing was the store and house of Sylvanus Davis, the principal trader of Falmouth. Near the corner of Fore and India Streets was the public house of Richard Seacomb, licensed in 1681 to operate this one-of-a-kind establishment. In May the following year he was fined fifty shillings for selling liquor to the Indians.

Fort Loyall consisted of a number of low buildings surrounded by an outer-barrier palisade fence supporting wooden observation towers. The half-acre site was defended by eight cannon. Garrison houses were built in other parts of Falmouth that were reinforced to be used as places of refuge. One was located at the top of Munjoy Hill near the present observatory, one at the bottom of the present Exchange Street, and one on the present Free Street.

The tiny town remained peaceful and began to thrive as demand grew for its products. Fate, however, was soon to step in: in 1688 King William's War with France erupted. King Louis XIV was at the height of his career and desirous of world control. He had placed Count Frontenac, the greatest of Canadian governors, in charge of French-American affairs. He organized a campaign to conquer all the English settlements and place them under French control, even then considering the Casco Bay area to be the natural seaport of the Canadians.

So America became a battleground, and little Falmouth was soon to feel the destructive effect of the French and their Indian allies as the French began to carry out Count Frontenac's ambitious plans.

Things began to heat up in 1688 when Boston sent an expedition to French-controlled territory in the Province of Maine in an attempt to rout a French nobleman, the Baron de St. Castin, who had settled on the Penobscot and married the daughter of Chief Madockawando, thereby earning the devotion of the tribe. Cotton Mather, pastor of the Second Church of Boston, referred to St. Castin's followers as the worst sort, "Half t'one and half t'other, half indianized French and half Frenchified Indians."

Baron Jean-Vincent de St. Castin, portrayed here by Charles E. Banks in 1890, served in the French military in Acadia in the early seventeenth century. Married to a Penobscot Indian, he fought many battles against the English for dominance of the Province of Maine between 1665 and 1712.

The baron responded in 1689 by leveling the fort at Pemaquid and sending a French and Indian force southward toward Falmouth. Town residents began to call for assistance, and this time Boston responded by sending short, stout, fifty-year-old Major Benjamin Church to their aid. With his hair styled in tight ringlets, he looked more like a preacher than a famous Indian fighter. Church had gained his fame when he ended King Philip's War in 1676 by killing King

Philip, or Metacomet, at Rhode Island's Great Swamp Fight. In his memoir *The Entertaining History of King Philip's War,* Church refers to himself as "a person of uncommon activity and industry."

Early in September, Indians had already begun gathering in the vicinity of Falmouth. and one resident of the town had noticed a large group of over two hundred on what is now Peaks Island. On Friday, September 20, two sloops sailed into Falmouth Harbor carrying Benjamin Church and two hundred Massachusetts volunteers and their Indian allies. His orders read, "The company shall have the benefit of the captives and all lawful plunder and the reward of eight pounds per head for every fighting Indian man slain by them." Already anchored in the harbor was a Dutch ship with a female passenger on board who had been recently ransomed from Indian captivity. She informed Church that she had seen at least eighty canoes and had been informed by the Indians that there would be at least seven hundred men in the force.

The population of Falmouth at the time was made up of only about twenty-five families, most of them clustered in their houses around the woefully underarmed Fort Loyall, which was useless in facing the largest force of Indians in the Province of Maine's history. Under cover of darkness, Church landed his men and scattered them between the fort and nearby houses. When dawn broke, Anthony Brackett was in his orchard at Brackett's farm on the other side of the peninsula. He noticed dozens of canoes sailing toward him and heard the clatter of musket fire. The Brackett farm was on land that is now Portland's Deering Oaks.

At sunrise Church sent his men toward the farm across the peninsula, only to be informed by Brackett's sons that their father had been killed and their orchard overrun by Indians. To make matters worse, word came from Fort Loyall that bullets stored in casks there were too big to fit their muskets. Church dashed back to the fort and ordered all the bullets to be dumped on the grass and hammered into a useful size. Returning rapidly toward the battle carrying three knapsacks of powder and bullets, he found himself stranded by the rising tide on the wrong side of a stream that was part of Back Cove. Fortunately, a loyal Indian ally from King Philip's War called Captain Lightfoot was nearby, and he saved the day: putting the powder on his head and carrying the bullets, he swam the stream with the much-needed supplies.

Finally, eighty of Church's men, divided into two companies, were able to make it to the other side. Church himself had discovered a small bridge nearly a mile away and decided to attack the Indians from behind. When he finally succeeded in crossing, he found "the enemy just gone, the ground being much tumbled with them behind." By this time low in ammunition, Church spotted the Indians heading back toward town and gave chase as far as Munjoy Hill. Seeing nothing more than cattle grazing quietly, Church and his men made their way back to Brackett's farm. The Indians had gone, vanishing as quietly as they had arrived.

The sun was setting as Church marched his men back to Fort Loyall carrying their casualties. In all, there were eleven wounded and ten dead, including Anthony Brackett, George Bramhall, and an African American, one of the first black soldiers mentioned in Maine's history. The Indians had left nothing behind but litter. They had carried all their dead and wounded with them.

The battle had lasted from sunrise to sunset, the English coming out on top. Church and his two hundred men had successfully turned back a superior force of some seven hundred Indians, but the next time the call for help came from Falmouth it went unanswered. Church's next visit to the town would be for an entirely different and more gruesome reason.

The site of the Battle of Deering Oaks is little known by the people of Portland today; as they drive by the beautifully landscaped park, they often miss the small slate tablet on a tree that marks the spot where the largest battle in Portland's long history was fought.

After the battle Church informed the town's residents that he was returning to Boston. They, in turn, fearful of another attack on the town in the spring, immediately implored the major to take them with him in his ships. Instead, he promised to tell the Massachusetts government of their fears and was hopeful that he and his volunteers would be able to return in the spring. Unfortunately for Falmouth, because of other pressing government concerns, Church was unable to get a hearing on their request for aid and finally returned to Plymouth, Massachusetts. In February 1690 he returned to Boston and presented a written statement to his superiors informing them of Falmouth's danger of further Indian attack. As far as Church was concerned, he had fulfilled his promise to the people of Falmouth, and, as he put it, he should thus be relieved of any responsibility for the loss of any future lives of the town's inhabitants.

The catastrophe that Benjamin Church had tried to warn Boston of was not long in coming. In March 1690 a group of Indians commanded by a French officer attacked and destroyed Salmon Falls. At this time, however, the provincial government was more concerned with aggression than with protecting the people living on the frontier.

An expedition was sent to Nova Scotia under the command of Sir William Phipps on April 28 to capture Port Royal. Meanwhile, a plan was being finalized at Quebec between French authorities and Baron de St. Castin of Penobscot and his Indian allies to take Fort Loyall and destroy Falmouth.

Early in April, at the eastern end of Casco Bay, a French and Indian rendezvous had taken place. A foraging party was sent from their hiding place to the vicinity of Falmouth, where they stole a number of cattle, probably to be used as part of a feast when St. Castin and his father-in-law, Madockawando, arrived with their forces. Early in May a fleet of canoes was spotted by some fishermen crossing the bay, probably from Jewell's Island. They hastily returned to Falmouth with the news, and on May 15 Lieutenant Thaddeus Clark and thirty men left Fort Loyall and marched to the top of Munjoy Hill, where they suspected the Indians were hiding behind a fence line. Thinking there might be but a small force there, they boldly attacked toward the fence, only to find the Indians well prepared and waiting. The results were horrendous. Lieutenant Clark and thirteen of his men were killed on the spot. The rest escaped to a nearby garrison until night fell and they were able to return to Fort Loyall.

A short time later the Indians turned their full force against the town, setting fire to all the buildings surrounding the fort and destroying all the garrison houses before turning their attention to the fort itself. Captain Sylvanus Davis, now in command of the garrison, left an account of the battle that is preserved in the Massachusetts Archives. He said a party of French from Canada joined by between four and five hundred Indians attacked at dawn on May 16, 1690. The battle raged for five days and four nights, as the enemy took advantage of a deep gully in front of the fort that was out of reach of Fort Loyall's guns. Inside, ammunition was almost gone and a majority of the defenders had been killed or wounded. Most of the town's residents had taken refuge inside the fort. Captain Davis wrote, "The 20th about three o'clock, afternoon, we were taken. They fought us five days and four nights in which time they killed and wounded the greatest part of our men, burned all the houses, and at last we were forced to have a parley in order for a surrender. We not knowing that there was any French among them, we set up a flag of truce in order for a parley. We demanded if there were any French among them, and if they would give us good quarter."

The answer was shouted back: they were indeed Frenchmen and would comply with Davis's request. But he had to make sure that not only his men, including the wounded, but also the women and children would be able to march to the next English town under protection before the surrender actually took place.

Davis asked the French commander to swear that these conditions would be met, and he agreed. When the seventy men and many women and children left in the fort finally came out and laid down their arms, they were seized by the Indians, who murdered many of the wounded and carried the others away. When Davis protested this breech of faith, he was told that he and his men were all rebels against King James II, who was under the protection of the French king.

Davis and three or four of his men were kept by the French as prisoners. Describing his captivity, he wrote, "After they had cruelly murdered our women and children and especially the wounded men, the French kept myself and 3 or 4 more and carried us over land to Canada. . . . about twenty four days we were marching . . . on land and water carrying our canoes with us. . . . I must say they were kind to me in my travels . . . our provision was very short; Indian corn and acorns—hunger made it very good & god gave it strength to nourish. I arrived at Quebec the 14th of June 1690, where I was civilly treated by the gentry." On October 15 Davis was finally exchanged for a French officer. He died in 1703.

About twenty of the Indians who attacked Fort Loyall had been captured during an earlier attack on the town and had been held at the fort as prisoners. They were eventually set free and, being familiar with the defenses of the fort and the area, had guided the group that destroyed Falmouth. The French and Indian attackers suffered only a couple of minor injuries. One Frenchman had his arm broken by a cannon ball, and an Indian was wounded in the thigh.

The bodies of all those killed at Falmouth probably remained where they had died, as there was no time to recover them after the fall of the fort. The townsmen who had fled before the battle went to Wells and safety, and the bodies of over one hundred of their neighbors were left to the mercy of the birds and beasts for two years. Finally, in 1692 Benjamin Church, on the way back to Boston from an expedition, stopped at Falmouth and buried the bleached bones of the dead that still lay where they had fallen, probably in a single pit at the foot of India Street.

# 2 resettlement and disaster

I can see the shadowy lines of its trees,
And catch, in sudden gleams
The sheen of the far-surrounding seas,
And Islands that were the Hesperides
Of all my boyish dreams.

*—Henry Wadsworth Longfellow, "My Lost Youth"*

AFTER THE DESTRUCTION and abandonment of Falmouth, it would be nearly thirty years before any permanent inhabitants began to venture back, despite the area's natural advantages. Most of the original streets that had been laid out had deteriorated to their natural

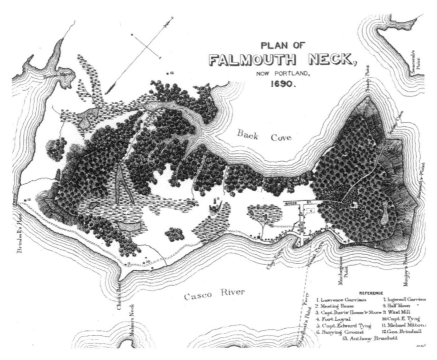

An early map of Falmouth Neck in 1690 shows a land dominated by forests and swamps, which dwarf the early English settlement.

state. The Indian wars had continued, but in Falmouth there was nothing left to attack. The history of the peninsula had been one of failure due largely to the constant turmoil and infighting over property rights and the inability of the common residents to gain a voice in the conduct of their own affairs. The entire province had been like a giant chessboard and its inhabitants pawns of rival governments and religions.

After the town was abandoned in 1690, a stockade was built in 1700 at the mouth of the Presumpscot River in what is the present-day town of Falmouth. The settlement was called "New Casco," as opposed to "Old Casco," one of the names of the abandoned settlement. The new fortification was simply called the Casco Fort; it was 250 feet long and 190 feet wide, with small watchtowers at the rear and larger ones facing the water. Inside were a number of buildings, including a magazine and a blockhouse. The primary use of the new fort, which was to be a neutral place, was for trading with the Indians, who had come to depend on the white man's wares. In spite of its supposed neutrality, the Casco Fort was attacked after the beginning of Queen Anne's War in 1703, and in 1716 was ordered demolished by the Massachusetts government and all stores belonging to the settlers removed.

There had been attempts to negotiate peace with the Indians, but they met with failure until July 1713, when Major Samuel Moody, then in command of Casco Fort, acted as a courier in talks between the Indians and the government, which finally resulted in the Treaty of Portsmouth.

After Casco Fort was torn down, the small number of inhabitants who had settled around it realized that their protection was gone and scattered to other parts of the province. Major Moody and one of his lieutenants moved to Falmouth Neck and built a fortified house at the present corner of Fore and Hancock Streets, where George Cleeve had first settled. Within two years, fourteen families had returned to the immediate vicinity. Meanwhile, some of the original settlers had begun to come back and reclaim their old property, now being used by new inhabitants.

The General Court appointed a committee to lay out town plots. In July 1718 the committee members traveled to Falmouth and sent a favorable report back to the legislature. Falmouth was reincorporated and old boundaries were located. On March 10, 1719, a meeting was held to organize the town, and officials were selected, as was a representative to the General Court.

Even though England and France had signed a peace treaty at Utrecht, Holland, in 1713, Indian attacks had not stopped because Canada hadn't given up trying to gain control and possession of New England. It wasn't until July 1727 that forty representatives from Maine, Massachusetts, and New Hampshire met on Munjoy Hill with a group of two hundred costumed Indians from various regional tribes at a site that is now the Eastern Promenade at the end of Quebec Street. Talks were held in a spacious tent where, after the successful negotiations were concluded, a sumptuous feast was held at government expense. The Reverend Thomas Smith, pastor of the First Parish, who kept a historically important journal throughout his long lifetime, noted that "the Indians appeared with French colors and made a great show." The peace talks constituted the largest assembly of people ever to gather in the town, and the inhabitants were ill-prepared to accommodate so many people, especially when it came to food and lodging. Once everyone had left town, according to Smith, "they left us quite bare and nothing of the country's produce left, only three bushels of corn and some small things." The peace treaty was beneficial to both parties and was followed by a long period of peace.

## *Peleg Wadsworth*

OCCUPATION: Teacher, businessman, soldier, farmer

LIFETIME: 1748–1829

FAMILY: Born in Duxbury, Massachusetts, to Peleg and Susanna Wadsworth. Married in 1772 to Elizabeth Bartlett; raised ten children, including daughter Zilpah, the mother of the poet Henry Wadsworth Longfellow.

ACCOMPLISHMENTS: Fought in Revolutionary War from the beginning, including the Battle of Long Island in 1776. Appointed brigadier general in 1777 and adjutant general of Massachusetts in 1778. Served as second in command during the Penobscot Expedition against the British at Castine, Maine, in 1779, which resulted in one of the worst American military defeats of the war—though it was Wadsworth's finest engagement. Named commander of all troops in the Province of Maine in 1780. Captured by the British the following year and imprisoned. Went on to serve seven terms in the U.S. Congress.

GREATEST CHALLENGE: Wounded during capture, he was imprisoned with another officer for several months but made a daring escape after cutting a hole in the ceiling of their jail and crawling over the heads of his captors during a thunder storm.

Peleg Wadsworth

*"The knowledge of men as well as letters is equally indispensable—The one must be attended to & the other not omitted. A man with moderate literary knowledge & good manners will make a much better figure thru the world than one with great science, with manners uncouth and disgusting. A person must be agreeable to be attended to."*

Beginning in 1724 many of the old streets were reestablished and new ones laid out. The old Broad Street, which ran from the water inland, was renamed King Street. In 1837 the name was changed again to the present India Street. Fore Street, on the waterfront, became the main business thoroughfare, and the old country road was named Back Street. It ran westerly from India Street; the part that ran east was called Main Street. Later the name of the entire street was changed to Congress Street. Middle Street, one of the earliest established, retains its original name and direction. As the town grew, other streets were laid out connecting the major east-west roads. Exchange Street, now the heart of the Old Port section, began as Fish Street; other streets received equally colorful names, such as Turkey Lane, Fiddle Lane, and Love Lane.

Fore Street in Portland in the late 1840s, when it still served as the city's waterfront. The domed building is the old Custom House.

Although some of the earlier profitable business opportunities were now gone, taken over by the Canadian French, other opportunities arose. The rich fur trade was confined almost entirely to Canada, while fishing faced strong competition from Newfoundland. Falmouth, however, was holding its own in the rapidly growing fields of shipbuilding and commerce, and the lumber business was still thriving.

Fishing boats dry their sails in Portland Harbor in 1895.

The population began to spread to interior sections, where farms and villages were established. Along the harbor general business and water transportation were developing and gaining importance of their own. Another important factor in the growth of Falmouth was the neglect of England, which in turn grew into opportunity for all of America. Without realizing it, this country was making progress toward independence.

By 1719 Falmouth residents turned their attention to religion and began looking for a minister. The town gave the job of finding one to Samuel Moody, and they voted to pay fifty-five pounds for his support. Finally, a young Harvard College graduate, Jonathan Pierpoint, was named to the position in 1721. A new meetinghouse had been begun the previous year, but work progressed slowly, and it wasn't until 1725 that the building at the corner of India and Middle Streets was finally enclosed.

The Massachusetts General Court had established all of Falmouth as one parish, and it remained that way until the Cape Elizabeth portion of the town became a parish by itself in 1737. Stroudwater and New Casco followed, creating a total of four parishes.

Ecclesiastical destiny found Falmouth in 1725, when the twenty-three-year-old Reverend Thomas Smith arrived as a visiting preacher. Returning to town periodically to give his sermons, he impressed the town-folk enough that they offered him the post permanently. After nine months of deliberation, Smith finally decided to accept the town's offer of a seventy-pound salary, plus board, and on March 8, 1727, he became the first regularly ordained minister in Maine east of Wells.

The following year he married Sarah Tyng, the first of three wives and the mother of his eight children. They lived in the first substantial house built on the peninsula. It was forty feet long and twenty feet wide, with a kitchen in the rear. According to Portland's premier historian, William Willis, it was "the best house in the village for many years; as late as 1740 it contained the only papered room in town, and this, by way of distinction, used to be called the papered room; the paper was put on with nails and not by paste."

Reverend Thomas Smith

Throughout his long life Smith was active in both public and church affairs, and he is important to Portland because of his personal journal; his daily entries of current events do much to disclose the history and development of the town. Smith had a practical business talent and speculated in real estate. He bought land from the Munjoy title and other claims of the old properties. By 1742 his efforts included his mansion house and barn on three acres of land and a number of large lots adjoining his original holding. There were about sixty acres on the Neck and one-third of both Peaks and House Islands as well as parts of six other properties. He also owned shares in various of his family's estates that he had inherited.

Thomas Smith remained the pastor of the First Parish Church for sixty-eight years. He lived in his house on Congress Street until it was destroyed in 1775 by the British during their bombardment of the town. During the Revolutionary War he offered his one black slave to the army after having him sign a document that guaranteed his freedom after the war on the condition that he split his soldier's pay with Smith.

Smith died on May 25, 1795, at the age of ninety-four; he was succeeded by the associate pastor, the Reverend Samuel Deane, who, fortunately for Portland, also kept a daily journal.

Travel in colonial Falmouth was difficult and it was carried out mainly on foot or by horseback. The roads in town were terrible, and outside the town the roads were almost nonexistent. One road wound along the shoreline, intersected along the way by many streams that could be crossed only by ferries. The most common means of travel in and out of the area was by boat.

The difficulty of travel and the wide separation of houses led to the slow development of education in the area. This and the constant worry and danger of possible Indian attacks held parents back from fulfilling this obligation. It wasn't until 1733 that the first schoolmaster of record, Robert Bayley, was hired at a yearly wage of seventy pounds to instruct the children living on the Neck. Twelve years later, Henry Wadsworth Longfellow's great-grandfather would become the principal instructor at Falmouth, a job he would hold for fifteen years.

This was a period of slow but steady growth for the town. Trade with the sugar producing colonies of England, France, and Spain in the Caribbean and West Indies grew rapidly as did the importing and exporting of goods to and from these countries. Shipbuilding expanded as trade increased and became very important to coastal towns; soon Falmouth became the most prominent in the area.

# Edward Preble

OCCCUPATION: Naval officer

LIFETIME: 1761–1807

FAMILY: Born at Falmouth (now Portland), Maine, the son of Revolutionary War Brigadier Jedidiah Preble. Married in 1801 to Mary Deering. One son, Edward, and three grandchildren.

ACCOMPLISHMENTS: Ran away at age sixteen to become a privateer. Appointed midshipman on the frigate *Protector* two years later. Fought in two battles before being captured in 1781 and released a year later. Earned a reputation for undaunted courage during the war. After fifteen years in the merchant service rejoined the navy and advanced rapidly in rank. Became commodore of a seven-ship squadron in 1803 in the war against the Barbary pirates and inflicted severe damage and heavy casualties. Returned to the United States in 1804 to supervise the construction of gunboats. Died in 1807, just ten days after his forty-sixth birthday.

GREATEST CHALLENGE: Preble's strenuous training methods and bold thinking led to his influence over and the later successes of Stephen Decatur, William Bainbridge, David Porter, and others who served under his command at Tripoli.

Edward Preble

*"This is the United States ship* Constitution, *forty-four guns, Edward Preble, an American Commodore, who will be damned before he sends his boat on board any vessel."*

Even as the prospects of the town grew, there was nevertheless the constant shadow of threatened war and Indian attack. The French had never given up their claims of territory and had maintained communications with the Indians of Maine. Falmouth had some protection from the frontier settlements to the north that were beginning to grow: Buxton, Gorham, Windham, and Brunswick. But the oceanfront was dangerously exposed to aggression from the ships of France and Spain. Finally, in 1741 the Massachusetts General Court granted money for the building of a fort for protection of the shore and harbor. A regiment was raised and put under the command of Samuel Waldo of Falmouth, and blockhouses were set up at various locations.

The French meanwhile had been busy putting their fortifications in good order for offensive warfare. The situation was growing tense, and soon war was declared between England and France, which greatly alarmed all of New England, including Falmouth. Under the guidance of France, the Indians were again randomly attacking towns, which caused serious apprehension at Falmouth. Finally, the two war-weary countries had had enough, and in 1748 they signed the Treaty of Aix-la-Chapelle, thus ending the War of the Austrian Succession. At the same time there was a general peace agreement with the Indians, but as had been true in the past, it wasn't long before they again began attacking at random.

In 1756 warfare between England and France began once again, this time with America as the grand prize. Finally, on February 10, 1763, under the Treaty of Paris, France finally gave up its claims of ownership of American territory.

Before the Seven Years' War had begun, the population of all of Falmouth was estimated at about 2,700; the Neck itself claimed 720 persons, including 21 slaves and servants. Slavery was then legal and it remained so until it was abolished in Massachusetts in 1783. Nineteen years later the Neck's population had grown to about 1,000, and the Neck became the seat of business, it being the largest population center in the entire town of Falmouth.

A regular customs collection district was established in 1758 because of the large amount of foreign business done in the port. Francis Waldo was appointed the first commissioner, and his deputy was Stephen Longfellow, the poet's grandfather. Shipping became so important that it led to the growth of the shipbuilding industry and the opening of a number of shipyards. The first of these was built just east of India Street, and it remained in business for nearly a century.

The whole district of Maine had originally been considered to be one county, York. In 1760 the Massachusetts General Court organized two new counties, Cumberland, which still retains much of its original area, and Oxford and Lincoln, which took up the rest of the province. Falmouth became the county seat of Cumberland County.

Falmouth was flourishing by 1765, and fifty new buildings were built that year. Most of the population lived between India Street and what is now Monument Square, extending back to Congress Street. At both ends of the peninsula were wooded hills with level ground between them. Fore Street was then the waterfront, with numerous wharves jutting out into the harbor. The population was largely well-to-do and contented, the majority owning their own homes. Money was scarce, but a system of barter had been set up to ease the exchange of goods and services. Both public and private schools had been established. Churches not only served as places of worship but also were used for weekly social gatherings. Church attendance was compulsory. When winter came, however, attendance was not only compulsory but at times almost unbearable because of the lack of heat. Baptismal water and feet were often likely to freeze.

In 1760 a new king was crowned in England whose reign would lead to much discontent in Falmouth and throughout the colonies. George III was an arbitrary and bigoted monarch. It was the titled aristocracy and the upper class whose influence really directed many of the laws that would affect incomes and conditions in Falmouth. Their interests lay in trade and self-advancement, and new laws were geared to the aristocracy's interests. The Navigation Act and other trade laws not only were offensive to Falmouth businessmen but were causing serious financial difficulties there because they were, in effect, a prohibition of foreign commerce. Measures had to be taken to circumvent these odious laws, not the least of which was smuggling.

The British government, of course, had a reason for the passage of the trade laws; it claimed they were necessary to recoup the expenses incurred in the defense of the colonies—this, despite the fact that they had largely left the colonies to defend themselves. Gradually, resentment and discontent grew to the point where physical acts of rebellion and public demonstrations began to take place.

In 1764 Parliament acted to enforce the Sugar Act, which imposed steep duties on West Indies goods, something that dug deeply into the pockets of Falmouth businessmen, who were heavily involved in that trade. This was followed by the Stamp Act, which levied taxes on all forms of business

*Lemuel Moody*

OCCUPATION: Shipmaster and businessman

LIFETIME: 1767–1846

FAMILY: Born in Falmouth (now Portland). Married Emma Crosby in 1797 and had seven sons and three daughters.

ACCOMPLISHMENTS: Served as a waterboy during the Revolution-ary War at age ten and went to sea to begin his quest for a career as a sea captain at war's end. In 1799, while he was serving as cap-tain aboard the schooner *Betsy* on a trip to Surinam, his ship was boarded by French privateers, and Moody and his crew were taken prisoner. Back in Portland he formed the Portland Monument Ground to sell shares to finance his plan for erecting a signal tower on Munjoy Hill to alert shipowners of the approach of their vessels. In 1807 the Portland Observatory was completed; it became the focal point for com-munity gatherings after Moody built stables, a banquet hall, a dance hall, and a bowling alley at its foot and next to his own house.

GREATEST CONTROVERSY: Trying to collect for the loss of his schooner and cargo to a French privateer forty-three years after the event took place.

Lemuel Moody

transactions. Falmouth residents gathered together and marched to the customhouse, where they confiscated all the stamped papers they could find and burned them publicly.

In an effort to curb all the disobedience occurring in the colonies, England sent troops to Boston in 1767. The call for independence slowly

# William King

**OCCUPATION:** Merchant, shipbuilder, statesman

**LIFETIME:** 1768–1862

**FAMILY:** Seventh child of Richard King of Scarborough. Half brother of the statesman Rufus King.

**ACCOMPLISHMENTS:** Largely self-educated, he was a self-made man who became very successful in business and politics. Starting as a worker in a sawmill, he went on to open his own mill. Rapidly expanding in many directions, he became a shipbuilder and the largest merchant-shipping owner in Maine. He was a significant real estate investor and opened the first cotton mill in Maine. King served in both the Massachusetts House of Representatives and the Massachusetts Senate. He became a major general of militia in charge of the Maine district in the War of 1812. A leader in the movement for statehood for Maine, he was president of the Constitutional Convention. His popularity earned him election as the first governor of the new state in 1820.

**GREATEST CHALLENGE:** Appointed a special minister by President James Monroe in 1821 to negotiate a treaty with Spain that kept the United States from involvement in the Mexican struggle for independence.

William King

began to be heard, and after the Boston Massacre took place in 1770, it became louder and clearer. This only infuriated the British even more, and they became determined to coerce the colonies to their will. Many colonists, however, rapidly lost their friendliness and loyalty to the king, becoming even angrier and more determined to govern themselves. Not everyone in the colonies felt this way. Many of the upper class were content with their lives and remained loyal to George III.

By 1775 most of the general business in Falmouth had suffered. There was still some profitable trade going on, primarily from the rapidly declining exportation of masts to England for the king's naval and merchant fleets. By then the Lords of Admiralty had decided to use their fleet for suppressive force, and they authorized their commanders to use their own discretion.

One Falmouth resident engaged in the mast trade was Samuel Coulson, who was, as the Reverend Thomas Smith described in his journal, "very troublesome and a raging Tory." He commanded a ship in the merchant service, trading between Falmouth and England. Coulson had arrived at Falmouth Neck in 1770 and married a local girl. He returned to England a short time later and came back to the Neck in 1774, when he began building a large-mast ship at his shipyard near India Street. An embargo was in effect against anything that would help England militarily. The local Committee of Inspection had decided that any masts for the British navy were military supplies and that was what Coulson's new vessel would be used for. Meanwhile, a ship had arrived in the harbor loaded with rigging, sails, and supplies for the new ship, and the committee refused it permission to dock and unload. An angry Coulson, in turn, sent a message to Captain Henry Mowatt, commander of the British sloop of war *Canceaux*, appealing to him to sail to Falmouth to force the Committee of Inspection to allow the stores to be loaded onto his new ship.

While all this was happening, a message arrived from the Continental Congress with news of the Battle of Lexington and an urgent call for volunteers. A group of some six hundred poorly disciplined minutemen from towns around Falmouth answered the call, including a company from nearby Brunswick commanded by Colonel Samuel Thompson, a short, stocky man who was highly excitable and easy to enrage. His enemies called him "a violent highflying stuttering foolish fellow."

By this point Captain Mowatt had responded to Samuel Coulson's call for help and had anchored the *Canceaux* in the harbor, accompanied by two tenders. The next afternoon he and two of his men went ashore and decided to walk up Munjoy Hill, unaware that the company of fifty men from Brunswick had decided to camp among the trees on the hill. When Mowatt and his party approached the encampment, Thompson assumed they were there to spy on them and promptly arrested Mowatt. A short while later, some of the principal townsmen, learning of his capture, convinced his captors to release him. It didn't take long for the angry captain to return to his ship, raise anchor, and sail away. This would not be the last the people of Falmouth would hear from Captain Henry Mowatt. The next time they did it would be the beginning of one of the greatest disasters in Portland's history, precipitated largely by Thompson's arrest of Mowatt. In 1776 the Provincial Congress rejuvenated the state militia and its command structure and, in spite of Thompson's unpopularity, he was appointed brigadier general in charge of the entire Cumberland County militia.

Early in June, after a trading expedition, Samuel Coulson returned to Falmouth in another of his ships to pick up a load of masts that by then had been hidden by the townspeople. The Committee of Inspection again refused him permission to load, forcing him to leave without his cargo. The masts were never picked up and lay slowly decaying for the next sixty years.

The siege of Boston was then in progress, and Falmouth and surrounding towns raised companies that were sent to Boston to help George Washington, the new commander of the army, in the difficult task of driving the British soldiers from the city.

For a while, Falmouth experienced a period of relative quiet, although commerce had all but stopped. The quiet quickly turned to chaos and fear on October 16, 1775, when Captain Mowatt returned in the *Canceaux*. The Reverend Smith wrote, "A fleet of five vessels of war anchored at the island with Mowatt, a cat bomb ship, two cutter schooners, and a small bomb ship." Late in the afternoon the next day, an officer went ashore carrying a letter from Mowatt warning that the town was to be punished. Residents were given two hours to take what they could and leave. A three-person committee immediately rowed to the *Canceaux* and got Mowatt to agree to see if his orders to bombard Falmouth could be rescinded by the man who had issued them, Vice Admiral Samuel Graves. Mowatt told the committee that if the town agreed to give up all their arms, he would see what he could do.

Graves had ordered the punishment of the town after an attack by forty rebels on a small British sloop at Machias, Maine, the previous June. The order had included a number of towns, but weather conditions forced Mowatt to bypass them and head directly to Falmouth. Townspeople delivered a small number of muskets to Mowatt and were given a deadline of nine o'clock the next morning to deliver the rest. The whole town was now in a state of panic, and residents began loading wagons, carts, and wheel-

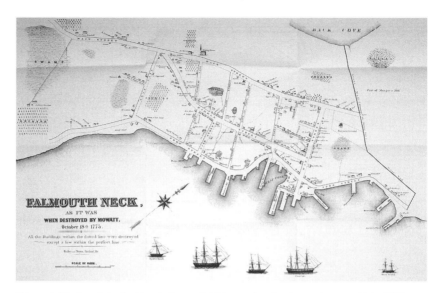

Falmouth Neck as it looked just before a British navy bombardment destroyed it in 1775.

barrows with whatever possessions they could save in an attempt to carry them to safety.

At nine o'clock on the morning of October 18, an angry and impatient Mowatt gave everyone thirty minutes to evacuate; exactly thirty minutes later a red flag was hoisted as a signal to begin firing. The first shots were purposely fired high as warnings, but then the bombardment began in earnest, as everything from grapeshot to red-hot cannonballs rained down on Falmouth Neck. Since most of the buildings were on level ground surrounding the waterfront, they were within easy range of the cannon, and soon a sheet of flames swept through the wooden buildings. Attempts by some of the residents to rescue their belongings proved futile because of the dangerous conditions. Parties of men from the ships were sent ashore to systematically torch the buildings that had escaped the bombardment because of the poor quality and shortage of cannonballs.

Smith's journal tells the story. "At nine A.M. they began and continued until dark, with their mortars and cannon, when with marines landing, they burnt all the lower part of the town and up as far as Mrs. Bradbury's excepting Mrs. Ross' two houses, and son Thomas' shop and stores, my house included. I rode to Windham just before the firing began, as did Mrs. Smith yesterday. A solemn time! . . . My house was the last that was burnt, though several times on fire, and not until near dark and kindled from

# Seba Smith

OCCUPATION: Lawyer, poet, writer, editor.

LIFETIME: 1792–1868

FAMILY: Born in a log house in Buckfield, Maine. Married to sixteen-year-old Elizabeth Oakes Prince in 1824. Raised six sons.

ACCOMPLISHMENTS: Despite limited opportunities for learning as a boy, he began teaching at eighteen. Entered Bowdoin College as a sophomore in 1815 and graduated with highest honors in 1818. Studied law in Portland, where he passed the bar, started practice, and began writing poetry. Became associated with the weekly *Eastern Argus* in Portland at age twenty-eight, first as an editor and then as joint owner. Started two nonpartisan papers in 1829, the *Family Reader,* a weekly, and the *Portland Courier,* the first daily newspaper east and north of Boston. Moved to New York in 1839 and edited three New York newspapers.

After a number of failures in the publishing business, retired to Patchogue, Long Island, and continued writing humor, poetry, and scholarly works. He is considered one of America's first political satirists.

GREATEST CHALLENGE: Overcoming early lack of educational opportunities to achieve prominence in writing and publishing.

Seba Smith

Capt. Sanford's [his next-door neighbor]." Smith returned to Falmouth about a month after the destruction to try to reestablish church services, but as he noted in his diary, "No lodging, eating or housekeeping in Falmouth."

The bombardment continued until six o'clock in the evening, destroying all of Falmouth Neck except for a few isolated buildings. One building just out of range of the cannon escaped. This was the one-story tavern of Alice Greele, a stubborn woman who stood by her building all through the day, more than once putting out fires as they started. Also gone were 130 houses, the Anglican church, the meetinghouse, the library, and the fire station. A great quantity of personal property was also destroyed because of the scarcity of horses, wagons, and other means of conveyance, along with all the confusion of the moment. A huge amount of furniture and other property was piled up in the streets and fields and left to the mercy of the flames, weather, and looters.

The town was not the only victim of Mowatt's revenge. There had been thirteen ships in the harbor at the time. Only two were captured, whereas eleven were sunk along with their cargoes. Falmouth had been reduced to blackened ruins; nearly two thousand homeless people faced the coming winter with nothing to look forward to except great hardship.

The historian William Gould in his book *Portland in the Past* tells the poignant story of one of the victims of the destruction that he heard as a boy.

> *The first tears I ever shed for public misfortunes were, I think, for suffering women and children of Falmouth. . . . This good woman who lived in the town . . . her husband had enlisted in the continental army, intending to leave his wife and child in their snug home in Falmouth. On the arrival of the ships, he was one of those who went to the islands to guard the cattle and sheep, and could not return until the firing had commenced. His name was Barton and he was then about twenty-eight and his wife about twenty years old. Mrs. Barton remained in the house waiting for her husband until the hot shell and shot began to fall near, and several of the neighboring buildings were on fire, and her own dwelling had become untenable. She could wait no longer. She tied up her only feather bed with some small articles of clothing in a sheet, and slung it over her shoulder. She then took her little boy on her other arm and fled from the burning town. To reach a place of safety she was obliged to walk nearly a mile through the most thickly settled part of the town with the ships in full view. Several times bombs with their smoking fuses fell near her, and she quickened her pace to escape the explosions. With many others she took shelter under the high ledges near the Casco Street church. . . . The vicinity was then a grove of oaks which gave Oak Street its name. A three-pound shot fell near her which she secured. Her husband found her on his return from the islands, and here they remained until nearly night. . . . Their dwelling and household goods were burnt and they were compelled to begin the world anew.*

Mrs. Barton died in 1841 at the age of eighty-six.

The burning of Falmouth caused widespread indignation throughout the colonies. When the news of the incident finally reached the Continental Congress, it did not go unnoticed in the debate for independence. While the debate was still in progress, the residents of the untouched section of Falmouth, off the Neck, held a meeting and voted to support the Congress if they decided to break from England.

Despite all the turmoil and destruction, Falmouth Neck was still the central point for the conduct of business, even though settlers could not be induced to return to stay because of the town's exposed situation. Travel was very difficult on roads that were really no more than trails, and communication was slow. The tavern that Alice Greele had saved from burning had become the headquarters for business and the assembly of military recruits. Civil government continued to operate, still in accordance with Massachusetts law.

The population estimate for the town of Falmouth in 1777 was seven hundred residents and as the Revolutionary War continued to drag on, conditions grew harder for them. Poverty and at times near famine persisted. Smith noted in his journal on July 31, 1778: "People fear a famine. The Indian corn curls and is like to come to nothing, and there is no prospect of any potatoes or turnips. . . . Lord have mercy upon us." Agriculture had suffered greatly because of the shortage of men to till the fields. Most of them were now serving in the army. In spite of this, the spirits of the people remained high, and the government took special notice of their patriotism.

By 1779 most of the campaigning in the war had moved southward, but conditions around Falmouth were still deteriorating. Nearly half the crops were lost because of a severe drought. And 1780 was no better. The lumber business and shipping no longer existed. Fishing was greatly limited by the British navy's policy of destroying all shipping that was not theirs. Even with all these deplorable conditions, Falmouth still contributed to the war effort with its share of men and supplies, including beef, shirts, shoes and stockings, and blankets. The Reverend Smith had done his share by sending his only slave, Romeo, to the army for three years.

Finally, on March 31, 1783, news was received in Falmouth that peace had finally come, and four days later the town expressed its joy with the firing of cannon from morning till dusk. ⌐

# 3

## progress and war

I remember the sea-fight far away,
How it thundered o'er the tide!
And the dead captains, as they lay
In their graves, o'erlooking the tranquil bay,
Where they in battle died.

—*Henry Wadsworth Longfellow, "From My Youth"*

AFTER THE SURRENDER of General Cornwallis and the coming of peace, Falmouth slowly began to draw its former residents back. A number of them who had fled during Mowatt's bombardment had set down roots elsewhere and did not return. New immigrants, however, began to arrive in large numbers to take their place.

A year after the peace treaty, fifty-eight houses and shops had sprung up, and an increasing number of people from Massachusetts and elsewhere came to live in the newly rejuvenated town. The first brick house ever to grace the peninsula was built in 1786 by Peleg Wadsworth, a former brigadier general in the war and the maternal grandfather of Henry Wadsworth Longfellow. He had become familiar with the area when he was appointed by George Washington as commander of the Province of Maine. After the war he had returned to Falmouth to seek his fortune. Built on Back (Congress) Street just up from the present Monument Square, the house still stands today, now the oldest house museum in Maine, and is part of the Maine Historical Society.

Falmouth Neck had always gotten along quite well with the rest of the town, but now the interests of the Neck began to differ materially. Rapid growth had made the Neck the center of business and commerce, and it was becoming inconvenient for those living farther afield to attend town meetings because of the distances some had to travel to get to them. There was also a great deal of jealousy developing between the Neck and the rest of Falmouth because of the growing prominence of the peninsula. As early as May 1783 a general meeting had been held on the Neck and a proposal put forth for separation of it from the rest of Falmouth. Although the proposal had been approved at that meeting, it was not followed through because of poor financial conditions at the time. It wasn't until July 4, 1786, that Falmouth Neck finally separated from the rest of Falmouth, and after much discussion it was given the name of Portland. The name was chosen because of the names of surrounding geographical features—Portland Head, Portland (Cushing) Island, and Portland Sound. The new town's boundaries were those of the Machegonne of George Cleeve, with the addition of land at the western end of the town. Its population had grown to about two thousand.

Surrounding sections of old Falmouth began to take on identities of their own. In 1776 Cape Elizabeth had been established as a separate town and included what is now South Portland. In June 1814 Westbrook became a town. The town was originally Stroudwater, but its name was shortly changed to Westbrook in honor of the king's first mast agent, Thomas Westbrook. Deering, now part of Portland, also became a town. The area that was left retained the name Falmouth.

Portland experienced rapid growth for two or three years but was then overtaken by a period of depression caused largely by the basic worthless-

# John Neal

OCCUPATION: Author and literary critic

LIFETIME: 1793–1876

FAMILY: Born on Free Street of Quaker parents.

ACCOMPLISHMENTS: Attended school until age twelve, when he left to enter business. Earned a living at many professions until he entered law school in 1815, where he began to write articles to support himself. Soon started to write novels under the pen name of "Jehu O'Cataract." Traveled to England in 1824 and returned to Portland in 1827 for a visit. Many locals found his writing offensive, so he decided to stay to prove them wrong. He spent the rest of his life in Portland, writing and reestablishing his law practice. He was an advocate of women's rights, prohibition, and temperance.

John Neal

*"'Verily, verily,' said I, 'if they take that position, here I will stay, till I am both rooted and grounded—grounded in the graveyard, if nowhere else.'"*

ness of the Continental paper currency. There was no circulation of a medium of dependable value, and a large number of business transactions were conducted using the old standby, barter. There was a slight increase in population and building during this period. In 1785 a small courthouse was built, with a whipping post and pillory in front for those who broke the law. A blockhouse jail stood nearby.

Shipping, which had disappeared during the war, slowly began to rebound. There was not one ship owned by a Portlander in 1787, but two years later tonnage had grown to over five thousand tons. With the growth of shipping came a need for aids to navigation, and in 1788 President

Washington authorized the funding of a new lighthouse to be built at Portland Head. Completed and finally lit in 1791, the lighthouse, it was soon discovered, was too short and difficult to see from the water. The height was adjusted until it became functional; it eventually earned its place as one of the oldest lighthouses in the United States. Thousands of visitors come to Portland Head Light by the busload each year, and it is probably the most photographed lighthouse in the country.

On April 30, 1789, the country's new constitution was finally ratified; there followed a period of progressive change. Portland advanced substantially as it grew under its new form of municipal administration.

From the earliest times, Portland had been open to hostile aggression from its unprotected coastline, but by 1794 the U.S. government had become concerned with coastal defense. Congress appropriated funds to build a fort on North Street at the top of Munjoy Hill, with an outlying battery on Monument Street. It was called Fort Sumner and mounted fifteen cannon that protected the entrance of Portland Harbor. The barracks were built on the summit of Munjoy Hill and surrounded by an earthen embankment with a deep, dry ditch at its base. The barracks and parade ground were within the enclosure.

Longfellow recalled the fort in his poem "My Lost Youth":

ABOVE: Portland Head Light, Maine's first lighthouse, was commissioned by George Washington and built in 1791.

BELOW: The clipper ship *Annie C. Maguire* was wrecked on the rocks at Portland Head Light on December 24, 1886, as it was headed into Portland Harbor following a trip to Buenos Aires.

*I remember the bulwark by the shore*
*And the fort upon the hill;*
*The sunrise gun with its hollow roar,*
*The drum-beat repeated o'er and o'er,*
*And the bugle wild and shrill.*

The fort remained active until after the War of 1812, by which time other forts had been constructed to complete the defense of Portland Harbor. Fort Preble was begun in 1808, and at about the same time Fort Scammel was built across the channel on House Island. Fort Gorges, the last of the protectors of the harbor's entrance, was not started until 1858. Named for the original owner of Maine, Fort Gorges was never manned and today stands in Portland Harbor as an empty, ghostly guardian of the city. All the forts ultimately became obsolete with the development of modern ordnance; they stand today as silent sentinels still on guard against unseen enemies.

As the nineteenth century dawned, Portland residents looked forward to quieter, more prosperous, and less tumultuous times. Little could they imagine that their future held more of what they had experienced during the previous two centuries. More turmoil and bloodshed would hang over their heads like ugly black storm clouds.

It began with the French Revolution in 1789. Three years later, after the king and queen were executed and the country became a republic, the rest of Europe felt it had an open invitation to declare war on France and turn

Fort Gorges sits in Portland Harbor, a guardian against possible attack. It was built shortly before the Civil War, in the 1850s, by order of Secretary of War Jefferson Davis. It was never manned.

# William Willis

OCCUPATION: Lawyer, historian.

LIFETIME: 1794–1870

FAMILY: Married to Julia Whitman, had nine children who predeceased their parents.

ACCOMPLISHMENTS: Considered the most important nineteenth-century Portland historian. Active in every aspect of the city's civic affairs for fifty years, including serving as state senator and Portland's mayor. Practiced law with Prentiss Mellen and William Pitt Fessenden. Successful in business, he became president of the Maine Central Railroad. His passion was the writing of history, and he was a frequent contributor to the daily press and scholarly journals. His greatest works were *The History of Portland, Journals of the Rev. Thomas Smith, and the Rev. Samuel Deane,* and *A History of the Law, the Courts, and the Lawyers of Maine.*

William Willis

the world into a war zone. Portland would become the beneficiary, as shipping and shipbuilding became the leading business because of the hostility between England and France and their allies. American ships were the only ones that could sail into European ports and were, as neutrals, free to sail where they wished.

The declaration of the new French Republic also affected Portland in a more social way. Portlanders expressed their sympathy toward France, and Francophilia became the rage. French fashions, manners, and language

The Battle of Tripoli, August 1804, in an engraving by John B. Guerrazzi, ca. 1805. The USS *Constitution*, in the right foreground, was the flagship of Edward Preble, the expedition's commander. Henry Wadsworth, the uncle of the poet, was killed in the battle.

became almost a mania, and only the influence of President Washington kept America from entering hostilities on the side of the French, who had, after all, come to our aid in our time of need during the Revolution.

It didn't take long for the windfall growth in trade to turn Portland into a very prosperous town with the most experienced seamen and officers in the country. One of the officers was Commodore Edward Preble, who commanded the USS *Constitution*, better known as "Old Ironsides." Preble led an expedition to Tripoli, where his squadron forced the feared Barbary pirates into submission, putting a halt to their demands of tribute from the world's shipping.

The rise of Portland's fortunes not only affected commerce and business but also led to a growth in population and the number of merchants. The town was becoming a pleasant place to live and raise children, as churches, schools, and a public library were erected. Building lots were going for as much as twenty dollars an acre. There was even a post office, although the bad roads out of town limited the amount of business done. Deliveries were scarce, and it took four

Old Ironsides docked at the Maine State Pier in a 1931 visit to Portland.

# John Brown Russwurm

OCCUPATION: Newspaper publisher

LIFETIME: 1799–1851

FAMILY: Born in Jamaica of a Creole woman and a white American father.

ACCOMPLISHMENTS: When Russwurm's father returned to the United States in 1807, John was sent to Canada for schooling. His father's new wife, Susan Blanchard, brought John to their Portland home on Ocean Avenue to be fully educated. In 1826 he graduated from Bowdoin College, becoming one of the first blacks to graduate from any college. (At the time, anyone with even a small percentage of African blood was considered black.) One year later he moved to New York, where he founded *Freedom's Journal,* the first black newspaper in America.

GREATEST CHALLENGE: Russwurm at first opposed black emigration to Liberia but later changed his mind, and at the end of 1829 he settled there. He became superintendent of schools and edited the *Liberia Herald*. He became governor of Maryland-in-Liberia, the African settlement sponsored by the Maryland Colonization Society. Russwurm left a clear mark on African American history.

John Brown Russwurm

days for letters to come from Boston. After 1800 stagecoach routes slowly began to appear and the post office finally began to grow in importance.

The establishment of Portland's first bank came in 1799. The Portland Bank was chartered by the State of Massachusetts with a capitalization of $100,000. The second bank, The Maine Bank, followed in 1802 with a capitalization of $150,000. Portland had become an affluent town with little or no poverty. The quality of life was superior to that of any earlier time, but the dark clouds were quickly beginning to gather, and it wouldn't be long before there would be a reversal in the community's fortunes.

Manufacturing was in its infancy. Most of the products needed by Portland's citizens were shipped from foreign countries. The United States grew from a strip of states along the Atlantic coast to include the land between the coast and the Mississippi River in 1803, as a result of the Louisiana Purchase. American ships were able to fill this demand for a while because of this country's neutrality by carrying cargo to and from both England and France. But in May 1806 England declared a blockade of all ports in Europe and the Indies in an attempt to weaken its enemy. Trade by neutral countries was effectively stopped by the harsh penalties of capture and confiscation imposed by Britain. American ships had little chance of delivering their cargoes because English ships stopped those vessels whenever they pleased, often impressing many of the crew into service with the British navy.

Napoleon, in retaliation, ordered all European ports closed to England and its allies, which made the American situation even worse. President Thomas Jefferson and the American Congress responded with their own Embargo Bill in December 1807, which not only prohibited all ships in U.S. ports from setting sail to any foreign port but also forbade even coastal and river trade. It was a drastic move that resulted in complete disaster, especially for the commercial town of Portland. Ships lay rotting at the wharves. Prices plummeted as products lost their value. William Willis in his *History of Portland* vividly described conditions: "Mercantile business came to a standstill. Eleven of the strongest commercial houses stopped payment in 1807 and this was followed the next year by nearly all of the rest. The shipyards were idle. Workmen found no employment. The grass literally grew upon the wharves. There were street parades displaying emblems of protest. A large meeting of the inhabitants was called and a committee chosen to devise a plan for the relief of the distressed poor of the town. At the market house in Monument Square a cooking range of large kettles was built and there hundreds, many of whom had been living in affluence, obtained the greater part of their daily food."

The Reverend Samuel Deane, who replaced Thomas Smith as pastor of the First Parish Church after his death, also kept track of Portland's history in his journal. He described Portland's plight during the dark period of the embargo with the simple phrase "Soup charity begins." The entry continues: "The distresses of the people, in consequence of the commercial restrictions of the 1807 embargo act[,] fell very severely upon this town; the failures and the stagnation of business threw a large body of industrious persons out of employment, and aggrevated the sufferings of the poor; it was said that two of the failures before mentioned deprived three hundred, besides sailors, of the means of subsistence: The poorhouse was crowded, and hundreds were denied even that provision, and it became necessary to resort to other means to prevent starvation. To this end, a soup house was established, where soup of an excellent quality was daily served out to the destitute at no expense to them."

From the end of the Revolutionary War to the Embargo Act of 1807, Portland had enjoyed uninterrupted prosperity. The population had grown from 1,500 to 7,000. The few dwelling houses that were left standing after Mowatt's bombardment in 1775 had increased to 670 at the end of 1806, many of them brick and costing as much as $20,000. As an indication of the depression of property values during the embargo period and the failures of their owners, many of these houses were sold for as little as $3,000 or $4,000.

By 1809 pressure on the government had grown to such a large extent that the Embargo Act was repealed and replaced by a new law called the Non-Intercourse Act. Although trade with England and France was still forbidden, it was now allowed everywhere else, and the profitable West Indies business was reopened. England, however, did not cease its practice of stopping American ships and removing some of their crewmen. By the beginning of 1812 over six thousand of our seamen had been impressed by the British, a situation that demanded a response from this country. It came on June 18, 1812, when Congress declared war against England.

Portland began building ships once again, this time sending them out as privateers. These fast ships were generally built by groups of investors who formed companies to reap the profits realized from the capture of enemy vessels. Captured ships were brought into Portland, where they were sold and the proceeds divided among the owners.

# Jeremiah Hacker

OCCUPATION: Reformer, journalist.

LIFETIME: 1801–1895

FAMILY: Born in Brunswick, Maine, to a large Quaker family.

ACCOMPLISHMENTS: Moved to Portland as a young adult and worked at various jobs, including shopkeeping, until 1841, when he became an itinerant traveling preacher. Returned to Portland in 1845 and began publishing a reform journal with the unusual title of the *Pleasure Boat*. Became well known as a journalist who spoke out against everything from organized religion to slavery, warfare, and the treatment of juvenile offenders in adult prisons. He was very influential in the building of a Maine reform school. His journal enjoyed widespread circulation until the beginning of the Civil War, when he lost many readers because of his pacifism. He eventually retired to New Jersey and a life of farming.

GREATEST CONTROVERSY: His outspoken radical stands against the popular feelings of the day.

Jeremiah Hacker

*"Ask your physicians if they can name five men and five women, even in the religious societies, that are fully qualified to produce healthy children."*

James Osborne painted the brigs *Enterprise* and *Boxer* exchanging gunfire off the coast of Portland in Casco Bay, September 5, 1813. Smoke from the battle was visible to Lemuel Moody from the top of the Portland Observatory; he relayed reports to the crowd of residents gathered below.

Much of the War of 1812 bypassed Portland except for one famous incident that took place about forty miles from the town on September 5, 1813. The whole affair started when the commander of the sixteen-gun British brig HMS *Boxer,* Captain Samuel Blyth, fired a few shots at an American privateer, the brig *Margaretta.* When the news of this incident reached Portland, it did not go unnoticed by the captain of the USS *Enterprise,* anchored in Portland Harbor. Twenty-eight-year-old Lieutenant William Burrows was not a man who was happy with his lot in life. He had gone to sea at age fifteen with Commodore Edward Preble aboard Old Ironsides and sailed to Tripoli for the fight against the Barbary pirates. He was an ambitious man whose career seemed to be at a standstill. He had been passed over for promotion until finally given command of the *Enterprise* just two months earlier, and when the news of the *Boxer's* action reached him, he decided to set sail to engage the enemy. The *Enterprise,* one of only forty ships in the young U.S. Navy, had come to be known as the "Lucky Little *Enterprise*" because of its success in capturing even more prizes than Old Ironsides.

By 5:00 A.M. the *Enterprise* had reached Pemaquid Point, where Burrows saw a suspicious ship hugging the shore. At 8:30 A.M. it finally raised the British flag and fired a shot toward the *Enterprise,* which then headed for the open sea, drawing the *Boxer* in pursuit. About nine miles west of Monhegan the wind died, becalming both ships for six hours. Finally, at about 3:00 P.M. the wind rose and the *Boxer* and the *Enterprise* sailed toward each other until they were only about two hundred feet apart. The next fifteen minutes saw both ships firing broadsides at each other. One from the *Enterprise* killed Captain Blyth. Five minutes later, Lieutenant Burrows fell when a sniper's bullet tore through his body.

The battle raged on until 3:45 P.M., when the British finally surrendered and the sword of the dead Captain Blyth was presented to the mortally wounded Burrows, still lying on the bloody deck. His death came eight hours later in his cabin, where he had been carried after the surrender.

During the short battle, a large crowd had gathered at the observatory to see the smoke from the cannon fire, the only evidence that war had come to the area. Actually, the only person able to see the smoke was Lemuel Moody, the observatory's builder, who had climbed to the top and used his

The artist Charles Frederick Kimball portrayed the graves of Lieutenant William Burrows, captain of the USS *Enterprise,* and Captain Samuel Blyth of the HMS *Boxer.* The men were killed during the famous Battle in Casco Bay in 1813. The men were buried side by side in Eastern Cemetery.

telescope to observe the puffs of smoke. He passed the news to the citizens gathered below, who cheered his account. Although the battle lasted only forty-five minutes, the toll was heavy. The number of British casualties was never clear because most of their dead, perhaps as many as twenty-five, had been thrown overboard. There were sixty-four prisoners, including seventeen wounded. The *Enterprise* had suffered thirteen wounded and only one death, Lieutenant Burrows's. Damage to the ship was relatively light, and it towed its badly damaged adversary into Portland, where the *Boxer* sat at Union Wharf until it was sold at auction. It was repaired and became a merchant ship until the end of its life in 1845. The *Enterprise* sailed on until 1823, when it was shipwrecked in the West Indies.

A dual funeral was held for the captains of the *Boxer* and the *Enterprise* on September 8, 1813. The historian Herbert Adams described the proceedings in an article in the *Maine Sunday Telegram:* "Hundreds lined the shores on Sept. 8 as the remains of Burrows and Blyth were borne to Union Wharf by twin barges rowed with measured strokes by merchant captains, as minute guns fired alternately from the Boxer and the Enterprise, and a solemn music was performed by a full band . . . twin mahogany coffins, draped in their tattered ships flags, were marched with muffled drums through hushed streets to the Second Parish Meeting House." The procession, accompanied by a large number of officials and citizens and by the sounds of gunfire, proceeded to Eastern Cemetery, where the bodies of the two heroes were laid to rest side by side. ᔕ

# 4

## statehood and expansion

ON THE DAY BEFORE CHRISTMAS 1814, peace with England finally came with the signing of a treaty at Ghent. Both America and England had grown weary. Napoleon had been defeated and was exiled to Elba, and the British had finally reached the point of exhaustion.

Through the war, Portland had been growing. With water trade cut off and communications interrupted, efforts were made to improve and construct interior highways. Because the importation of foreign goods had

The site of the graves of twenty-one soldiers from the War of 1812 buried at the Eastern Promenade. Captured at the Battle of Queenston, they died in Portland while on their way to Boston to be exchanged.

been blocked, new home industries had been developed that changed the character of the town to a place of general commercial importance rather than just a seaport. By 1815 the population had grown to over eight thousand residents. Factories of all sorts had sprung up, and Portland was now manufacturing tin plate, brass and iron, watches and clocks, furnaces for casting iron, and other necessary goods.

Confidence was growing, and so was the movement to separate Maine from Massachusetts. The embargo and the War of 1812 had deprived many Americans of their employment, and a large number of them emigrated to Maine, where virgin forests and open fields offered plenty of opportunity to earn a living. Unoccupied territory was opened up and new towns incorporated. Soon after the conclusion of the war, Maine's population reached nearly a quarter of a million, and six new counties were organized.

In 1816 about a hundred towns petitioned the Massachusetts General Court for a separate government for Maine. The court ordered each town to hold a referendum on the matter. When the voting was completed, the results showed a majority in favor of the separation. A bill was approved and again was submitted to the people, who needed a five-to-four majority for ratification. It was approved by a small plurality, not the majority that had been required, and it wasn't until June 19, 1819, that both houses of the Massachusetts legislature passed a bill setting forth the terms of separation and again submitted it to the voters of Maine. This time it was approved by a majority of two and a half to one.

On October 11, 1819, a convention was called to draft a state constitution. The delegates met at the courthouse in Portland and after some controversy, it was decided to call the new state Maine. After approval by the voters, the constitution was adopted and sent to Congress. Congress combined Maine's request with that of Missouri, as part of the Missouri Compromise, and statehood finally came on March 15, 1820.

The first state legislature met on May 31, 1820, in the courthouse in Portland, the capital of the new state, an honor it would hold until 1832,

# Neal Dow

OCCUPATION: Businessman, soldier, temperance advocate

LIFETIME: 1804–1897

FAMILY: Born to Quaker parents, he married Cornelia Maynard and had one son.

ACCOMPLISHMENTS: Became interested in the temperance question at an early age and went on to become a leader in the movement to ban alcohol. Served as mayor of Portland and as a member of the Maine Legislature. As mayor, in 1851 he drafted and had passed by the state legislature a bill prohibiting the manufacture and sale of intoxicating liquors, an act that ultimately led to the prohibition of alcohol throughout this country. He entered the Civil War as a colonel and was later commissioned a brigadier general. After the war he traveled throughout Europe promoting temperance and, upon his return to the United States, kept up the cause.

GREATEST CHALLENGE: Wounded twice in the attack on Port Hudson and captured, he was taken to the infamous Libby Prison, where his health was broken by lying on the bare floor during an exceptionally cold winter. He was finally exchanged after eight months and resigned from the army at the end of 1864.

Neal Dow

when the capital was moved to Augusta because of its central location. The first order of business was to name a new governor, and William King of Bath was chosen for the one-year post. Portland's population in 1820 had grown to 8,581, and that of the state as a whole had grown to nearly 300,000 living in 236 towns and 9 counties. Over the next ten years Portland continued to grow; according to William Willis, in 1830 there were 1,076 houses, 280 stores for the sale of merchandise, 305 offices and shops, 119 warehouses, and 8 factories.

*Nathan Clifford*

Nathan Clifford

*"Courts cannot nullify an act of the State Legislature on the vague ground that they think it opposed to a general latent spirit to pervade or underlie the Constitution where neither the terms nor the implications of the instrument disclose any such restriction."*

Travel south from Portland was made easier by the building of Vaughan's Bridge and the Scarborough Turnpike, which shortened the travel time between Portsmouth and Boston. Stagecoach service was begun and highway construction continued. In 1832 there were twelve stages that ran different routes from Portland. Five kept daily schedules, whereas others departed three times a week. Seven of them carried mail; the rest took passengers only. Express teams transported freight. The common points of departure were the Elm Tavern on the corner of Federal and Temple Streets and the Clapp Block on Congress Street. It took two days to travel to Boston, including an overnight stop in Portsmouth. The teams made up of four to six horses galloped into the front yards of numerous taverns along the route.

Many new public buildings were constructed in the years following the War of 1812. A new courthouse was built and later enlarged. It was a handsome building with a cupola; it served not only as a courthouse but also as the new State House. On a lot next door, a two-story building was constructed with apartments for the governor and state officers. The senate held its sessions on the second floor. This pedestal- and pilaster-ornamented building was located at the upper end of Exchange Street. The courtroom was used as a meeting place for the representatives.

ABOVE: Maine was admitted to the Union in 1820. The first State House was built on Congress Street in the new capital of Portland. This painting shows the State House as it looked in 1832.

BELOW: Market Square in Portland, now Monument Square, ca. 1886. The old City Hall, erected in 1825, is in the center. The building was originally used as a military hall and was remodeled in 1832 to become Portland's first City Hall. It was torn down in 1888.

In 1825, on a lot in Monument Square now occupied by the Soldier's Monument, a spacious new City Hall was built. It was used not only as a place to conduct city business but also as a public market. The lower floor held shops that provided substantial revenue for Portland.

In 1831 a committee was named to prepare a city charter that was approved by voters at a town meeting and then sent to the state legislature for its approval. On April 30, 1832, a city government was set up under the provisions of the charter. The city was divided into seven wards with a board of seven aldermen and a twenty-one-member common council that named its chairman, Andrew L. Emerson, as Portland's first mayor.

Portland's population had now grown to fourteen thousand and was increasing rapidly. The city was thriving. In 1837, however, Portland as well as the rest of the country suffered when it was hit by a tremendous commercial crash, the worst ever experienced in the United States to that time. Specie payments came to a standstill, but Portland, despite large losses, still maintained sound general business conditions.

In the early years, any expansion on the peninsula extended only a short distance from the coast. Settlers who chose to move farther inland found that it was difficult to market their products because of rough trails and undeveloped roads. Horsepower and waterpower were the main means of transporting people and goods. Then, after years of experimentation, a new invention began to change things for the better. The steam engine lent itself to many uses when its worth in hauling heavy loads was discovered. Railroads and steamboats began to lead the country into the future.

The Boston and Maine Railroad was incorporated in 1833, but it would take nine years before its lines were extended into Maine. The first railroad leaving from Portland was the Portland, Saco and Portsmouth. Chartered in 1837, it finally became operational five years later, and in 1842 it began chugging the fifty-one miles to Portsmouth, New Hampshire.

Shortly after Maine achieved statehood, Portland's export market was growing rapidly, and it became necessary to find an effective way to move goods to and from the coast. Interest grew in digging a canal from the interior to Portland, but attempts to finance such a venture were unsuccessful. When the legislature chartered the Canal Bank in 1825, interest again was sparked, and a new effort was made to build a canal from Sebago Lake to Portland, to no avail. After a charter was issued to a group of merchants in 1821, fund-raising began in earnest and construction started in 1828. The route ran from Oxford County, through Sebago Lake, to Portland. Because of the 260-foot drop in elevation between the beginning and end, a system of twenty-seven locks was used. Finally, on June 1, 1830, with great fanfare, the Cumberland and Oxford Canal was officially opened. A route now connected Portland inland for some fifty miles by the use of specially built canal boats.

The Cumberland and Oxford Canal was short-lived. The expansion of the railroads made the transporting of goods through the canal unprofitable.

# Elizabeth Oakes Smith

OCCUPATION: Writer

LIFETIME: 1806–1893

FAMILY: Born in North Yarmouth, Maine, later moved to Portland. Married at the age of sixteen to thirty-two-year-old Seba Smith. Raised six sons.

ACCOMPLISHMENTS: Taught Sunday school for black children at age twelve. Began her writing career early. Exposed to slavery during a trip to South Carolina with her husband. After moving to New York, continued her writing career with the publication of many stories in various journals; received her first wide literary notice with her novel *The Sinless Child,* published as a serial in 1842. After attending a women's rights convention in 1850, became an advocate and wrote ten articles for Horace Greeley's *Tribune* entitled "Woman and Her Needs." Spent the next two years on the lecture circuit, traveling through the East and Midwest. After the death of her husband, continued writing but lived in dire financial straits; was forced to sell most of her library after contributing some of it to Bowdoin College and the Maine Historical Society. She died after a short illness at the age of ninety-seven and was buried next to her husband in Patchogue, New York.

GREATEST CHALLENGE: Forgotten by most, she suffered many family tragedies. One son was imprisoned during the Civil War for outfitting a slave ship; another died in a shipwreck.

Elizabeth Oakes Smith

They could be hauled by rail faster and more cheaply than by canal, which also had the disadvantage of having to close in the wintertime. By the late 1880s it was pretty much abandoned, and what nature did not obliterate, filling in did.

# William Pitt Fessenden

OCCUPATION: Lawyer

LIFETIME: 1806–1869

FAMILY: Married Ellen Maria Deering, had four sons.

ACCOMPLISHMENTS: Practiced law in Bridgeton, Bangor, and Portland. He was a Maine legislator and a member of the U.S. House of Representatives and served in the senate 1854–64 and again 1865–69. An early member of the Republican Party, he was opposed to slavery and served as chair of the Finance Committee. Between his senate terms Fessenden was Abraham Lincoln's secretary of the Treasury 1864–65. He died in Portland in 1869 and is buried in an unmarked grave in the family plot in Evergreen Cemetery.

GREATEST CHALLENGE: As a member of the Reconstruction Committee, Fessenden cast the deciding vote against the impeachment of President Andrew Johnson.

William Pitt Fessenden

The coming of the railroads became an important factor in Portland's economic growth. By 1872 there were sixty-five trains a day stopping in Portland, which aided the city's ability to become a major center for exportation. The railroad's explosive growth had led to the movement of people and goods in many directions to and from Portland. The Androscoggin and Kennebec, the Penobscot and Kennebec, the Kennebec and Portland, the York and Cumberland, and the Portland and Ogdensburg were a few of the various lines, most of them part of the Maine Central Railroad system.

There was one railroad system whose name would stand out in its importance: the Atlantic and St. Lawrence Railway. Its construction would turn Portland into the winter port for Canadian grain. The Canadian government issued a charter for the building of the railroad from Montreal to Portland on February 10, 1845, after much hard work by the visionary Portlander John A. Poor, who gave up his law practice so he could follow his belief in the important part the railroads would play in this country's future.

Despite the fact that Portland was one day closer to Europe than any other American port, the battle to bring the Atlantic and St. Lawrence Railway to the city was not easily won. Boston was also interested in all the profit it would reap if it became the winter port for Canadian trade, but the dogged determination of John Poor won the charter. Portland remained the terminal for Canadian grain well into the twentieth century.

Ground was finally broken for the project on July 4, 1846, in front of a large crowd of enthusiastic spectators. Seven years later, in 1853, all the track was finally laid and service began. After a short period of operation, the Atlantic and St. Lawrence Railway ran into financial difficulty. Its route was taken over by the Grand Trunk Railroad, and lease rights to the track were granted for 999 years. The new railroad needed to be connected with those traveling south, so in 1850 Portland voters approved a project to build the present-day Commercial Street. The new thoroughfare was to run a distance of nearly six thousand feet west from India Street and would be one hundred feet wide; it would have a twenty-six-foot section in the center reserved for railroad tracks.

From the time of its founding, Portland's waterfront had always been Fore Street, which followed the outline of the harbor. The bustling cobblestone street was the center of all waterfront activities. When two railroad terminals were built at opposite ends of the city, the Atlantic and St. Lawrence offered to pay for the construction of a street to connect them. Portland's responsibility was to take care of the fill and drainage. The huge landfill project that turned part of the ocean into Commercial Street cost $80,000.

In 1875 the Grand Trunk built the first of three huge grain elevators on the Portland waterfront. These grain storage facilities each held over 200,000 bushels of wheat. By the winter of 1899 nearly 22 million bushels of grain were arriving in Portland, and 58 percent of that was exported to foreign countries.

Two new industries dominated the waterfront in the 1840s. The first of these was an outgrowth of the West Indies trade and was started by forty-

LEFT: Grand Trunk Station, at the foot of India Street, was built in 1903 as the terminus of the Grand Trunk Railroad from Canada. The building was torn down in 1966.

RIGHT: The Grand Trunk Grain Elevator, pictured in 1898, stored wheat from Canada when Portland became the winter port for shipment of Canadian grain to the rest of the world.

year-old John Bundy Brown, a legendary entrepreneur, who opened a sugar factory in 1845. The factory, a huge, six-story, block-long building, was constructed on a scale never before seen in Portland. Brown had arranged for molasses shipments from Boston's largest wholesaler. His first attempts at converting molasses into granular sugar did not prove very successful, and he lost money faster than he made it.

Brown didn't give up, however, and he finally hired a chemist who developed a system of using steam power to do the granulation. The 1850 *Portland Directory* stated: "Recent machinery for refining by steam has been added to the works and Mr. Brown is now enabled to turn out superior qualities of the finer grades of sugar—white, straw colored and yellow. Sixty hands are employed in the establishment and an average of 100 barrels of sugar are made daily. The works are located near York Street, and in their rear is a spacious stone wharf with sufficient water at high tide for floating the largest class of vessels engaged in the West India trade." In 1855 the company built a massive, eight-floor building that covered nearly an acre.

The J. B. Brown Sugar Company factory on York Street was one of the country's largest sugar producers. This building was destroyed in the 1866 fire and later rebuilt.

The Brown Sugar Company was one of only three sugar factories in the country, its one thousand workers producing 250 barrels of sugar daily. Income was more than half a million dollars a year. After eleven profitable years, the Great Portland Fire in 1866 destroyed Brown's factory, but he wasted no time in building an even bigger factory with the help of insurance money. Unfortunately, Brown failed to keep up with the more advanced production methods being used by his competitors, and he was soon out of the sugar business.

Born in 1805, John Bundy Brown had grown up on a farm in Lancaster, New Hampshire. When he moved to Portland he worked as a grocery clerk for a dollar a week, but his great

John Bundy Brown.

business ability soon put him on a path to great wealth with a personal empire the likes of which Maine had never seen.

He established J. B. Brown and Sons, a company that grew into the largest bank east of Boston. He also built railroads, highways, hotels, and other buildings, which made him one of Portland's premier developers. Civic duties played a large part in John Bundy Brown's life as well, and he served on Portland's City Council, the state senate, and a multitude of executive boards. Brown believed in giving generously to many charities. The J. B. Brown and Sons Company is in business today, still family owned and still helping to develop Portland commercially and industrially.

The other industry that dominated the waterfront was the Portland

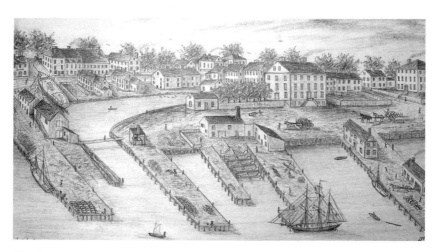

Clay Cove, an important commercial center at Hampshire Street near Middle Street, is shown in a Charles Goodhue sketch as it looked in 1840. It is now filled in.

Company. Established in 1847 by John Poor, whose enthusiasm for railroads included building his own locomotives, it developed a national reputation for constructing locomotives, boilers, and other machinery. The company, housed in a huge complex of brick buildings on Fore Street, also took advantage of the times by manufacturing shell casings and boats during wartime; it eventually diversified into automobiles, steam boilers, and just about any other machinery that would turn a profit.

The mid-1800s saw rapid and successful industrial growth in Portland. In 1849 a gaslight works was established; trans-Atlantic steamship service began; and a board of trade was formed in 1854. The labor supply was plentiful. The fact that Portland was the closest port to Europe was a great advantage, especially since freight rates were lower than in Boston and New York, its nearest competitors. Many of the city's products were widely used and were sold across the country and the world: canned goods, carriages, matches, glassware, sugar, brushes, paper, railroad iron, stoneware, chewing gum, shovels, furs, and straw hats. The historian Edward H. Elwell, in his 1875 book, *Successful Business Houses of Portland,* noted that Portland had a "worldwide reputation for packing companies that produced hermetically sealed provisions"—in other words, canned foods. Portland Glass Company, founded in 1864, attained a great reputation, even supplying Mary Todd Lincoln with glass dishes.

The city gained an early monopoly in the chewing gum industry when a factory for the production of spruce gum opened in 1852. The Zenas Thompson Company, established in 1854, was one of the few successful carriage makers in the country, building nearly a thousand carriages and fifteen hundred sleighs each year. Two hundred shovels were made each day by the Portland Shovel Manufacturing Company and shipped as far away

The Portland Company complex in 1938. The company was founded in the 1850s to make railroad locomotives, but it later expanded to manufacture everything from steam boilers to ships. The buildings are now used by a variety of businesses.

# Henry Wadsworth Longfellow

OCCUPATION: Language professor and poet

LIFETIME: 1807–1882

FAMILY: Son of Stephen and Zilpah Longfellow. Born and raised in Portland. Married to Mary Potter, who died of complications after a miscarriage, and Frances (Fanny) Appleton, who burned to death in 1861. He and Fanny had six children.

Henry Wadsworth Longfellow

ACCOMPLISHMENTS: Taught modern languages at both Bowdoin and Harvard Colleges. Became America's most popular and beloved poet with works that brought the plight of the world to the masses, such as "Paul Revere's Ride," *Evangeline: A Tale of Acadie,* and *The Song of Hiawatha.* By 1854 his fame and fortune had grown to the extent that he retired from Harvard and devoted the rest of his life to writing. His affection for his hometown never waned, and he visited frequently until his death. He commemorated his love of Portland in his poem "My Lost Youth."

*"The newspapers announce that I have resigned my Professorship. I have not yet; but have declared my intention so to do. There is something painful about the process; and I wish it were well over."*

GREATEST CONTROVERSY: His work in the translation of Dante's *Divine Comedy,* the first into English, against the wishes of his employer, Harvard.

Curtis and Sons, manufacturers of spruce gum, had a worldwide monopoly on its product. Some of the company's eighty employees are shown packaging the thousand-plus boxes that daily were shipped all over the country. The building still stands on Fore Street.

The front page of the first issue of the *Falmouth Gazette*, 1785. Maine's first newspaper was established to promote the separation of the province from Massachusetts.

as Australia. Hellman and Morrill Millinery and Straw Goods shipped their straw hats to New York and the Maritime Provinces. Portland Star Match Company was founded in 1866. After a slow start, primarily because of bad quality and an 1869 fire, things got better and the company grew to become the second-largest match maker in New England, and its matches were sold throughout the country and much of the world.

During the late eighteenth and early nineteenth centuries, Portlanders had a thirst for news, and a lively newspaper scene developed. From 1785 to 1835 a total of sixteen newspapers were published in Portland. The first paper in Maine was the weekly *Falmouth Gazette,* whose columns were filled with news and communications for and from many residents of the town. The first call for Maine statehood appeared in

Crowds throng Congress Street at the Eastern Promenade during holiday activities on July 4, 1898.

its columns in the February 5, 1785, edition in a poem referring to the rebuilt Falmouth as "the mistress of a rising STATE." It read, in part, "From the ashes of the old a town appears and Phoenix like, her plumy head she rears; Long may she flourish; be from war secure; made rich by commerce and agriculture; o'er all her foes triumphant; be content under our happy form of government; till (what no doubt will be her prosperous fate) herself the mistress of a rising STATE." (The *Gazette* presented the verses as prose.) The *Gazette* also printed the first published poem by Longfellow, written when he was thirteen and surreptitiously slipped under the paper's door. It was signed "Henry."

Portland was changing cosmetically. Both ends of the peninsula, largely open farmland, were developed into public parks. The eastern end at the top of Munjoy Hill became the Eastern Promenade, running more than a mile along the harbor and commanding an unsurpassed view of the harbor and the islands. Today it has evolved into a very popular playground for many of the city's families, who enjoy the promenade's bathing beach and walking trail. The other end of the peninsula became the Western Promenade, a park that stretches nearly three-quarters of a mile along the top of Bramhall Hill. It is a wide avenue with pleasing views of hills and mountains in the distance. Some of Portland's finest homes are built there.

# 5 portland diversifies

> "Build me straight, O worthy Master!
> Stanch and strong, a goodly vessel,
> That shall laugh at all disaster,
> And with wave and whirlwind wrestle!"
>
> —*Henry Wadsworth Longfellow, "The Building of the Ship"*

PORTLAND HAS BEEN AN ETHNICALLY diversified city from early in the nineteenth century, but the middle of the 1800s saw immigrants arriving in ever-growing numbers. The great Irish famine of the 1840s forced many Irishmen to leave their country as a matter of survival, and they headed for America—and Portland—in

Charles Goodhue sketched Portland's Munjoy Hill as it looked in the 1840s. Unlike today's thriving upscale East End community, the hill was then largely unpopulated. Portland Observatory is shown at the top of the hill.

numbers that greatly exceeded those of immigrants from other parts of the world who made their way here.

Within twenty years the Irish population had grown to two-thirds of the city's foreign-born; by 1860 the Irish made up 11 percent of Portland's total population of about thirty thousand. The major Irish settlement was at the bottom of Munjoy Hill. The more affluent families had homes on top of the hill. Another pocket of Irish lived in the Gorham Corner section, near the waterfront and the center of Portland. Many of them entered domestic service or became longshoremen.

Another group, small but no less important, includes blacks, who have been part of Portland's history since the first settlers came to the area. They arrived in large numbers just after the Civil War and more recently with the influx of Somalis, who have come to the city to escape the terrible war conditions in their country. Portland's chapter of the National Association for the Advancement of Colored People (NAACP) was organized in 1920, rechartered in 1960, and has been going strong since then.

Like the Irish, early black immigrants settled on and around Munjoy Hill. Some owned their own homes, but the majority rented. Religious activity was conducted at first in the Abyssinian Church on Newbury Street at the foot of the hill. It closed as a church in 1917 and after other uses was

# John Alfred Poor

OCCUPATION: Journalist, lawyer

LIFETIME: 1808–1871

ACCOMPLISHMENTS: Served as editor of the daily newspaper the *State of Maine* in Portland for several years, but his greatest achievement was as an active promoter of the current railroad system in Maine. Through his efforts, in 1845 Portland became the winter port of Canada; shipments of grain arrived from Montreal on the Atlantic and St. Lawrence Railroad, which was later taken over by the Grand Trunk Railroad.

GREATEST CHALLENGE: To convince the Canadian government to ship its grain to Portland instead of the competing Boston, Poor traveled alone by sleigh in a blinding blizzard in February 1845 to Montreal, where, at the last moment, he was able to convince the Canadians to award the contract to Portland.

John Alfred Poor

*"I was happily met with an attentive reaction and the idea seemed to take full possession of several number of the Board that any other Route than that of Portland would fail to secure to Montreal the great advantage of the trade of the St. Lawrence Valley."*

finally abandoned and boarded up. The building still stands, vacant and deteriorating, but there is hope for the future. It is now listed on the National Register of Historic Places, and efforts are under way to restore this important landmark, which once was a station of the Underground Railroad. Another important church was the AME Zion Church, later named the Green Memorial AME Zion Church.

Beginning in the 1860s many eastern Europeans, including Jews, began arriving, most of them from Russia and Poland. Like other immigrant groups, they tended to settle in the same area of the city, in a section bounded by India Street to the west, Commercial Street to the south, and Munjoy Hill to the east. Many of the Jewish immigrants opened small businesses and became important members of the business community.

From 1866 until 1904 there were no synagogues in Portland. Religious services were held in private homes until the first synagogue, Shaarey Tphiloh on Newbury Street, was organized by a group of twenty-five Jews. Soon small groups began to break away to form their own congregations, and other synagogues were opened on Congress Street and Cumberland Avenue. Then, as the city began to spread off the peninsula, many of the Jewish population followed. Synagogues were built farther away from the originally settled area, and the Orthodox religion began splintering into new, less Orthodox segments, each with its own place of worship. Today all three branches of the faith are represented, Orthodox, Conservative, and Reform.

Other immigrant groups were also important to Portland's population makeup: the French Canadians, the Chinese, and the Italians. The Italians did not become a significant part of Portland's population until the late nineteenth century.

The majority of Portland's Chinese immigrants came from Canton Province and entered this country on the West Coast, slowly migrating eastward. The first to arrive in Portland was a cigar maker named Ar Tee, who came in 1858 and opened a tobacco store on Federal Street. He became an American citizen in 1876 and in 1880 opened the city's first Chinese restaurant, on Commercial Street. As other Chinese made their way to Portland, they began to open their own businesses, including restaurants, shops, and laundries. The last Chinese laundry in Portland disappeared from the scene in 1966.

After Congress passed the first Chinese Exclusion Act in 1882, prohibiting Chinese immigration into this country, many Chinese began to enter illegally from Canada, and a brisk smuggling trade developed.

Shaarey Tphiloh Synagogue, shown ca. 1925, served as a center for the Orthodox Jewish community in Portland. It was located on Newbury Street until the congregation moved to a new building on Noyes Street.

One Portland resident, who operated her own laundry, attained national prominence in 1952. Toy Len Goon was named American Mother of the Year and was given a reception at the White House; she was then honored with parades in Philadelphia, New York, and Boston as she made her way back to Portland.

Besides becoming a haven for immigrants, Portland has also served as a major starting point for the new settlers who planned to move to other cities and states. House Island in the harbor became the Ellis Island of New England during the early twentieth century, as many foreigners arriving in this country first set foot there before continuing their journey elsewhere. House Island remained an immigration center until the beginning of World War I.

In the days leading up to the beginning of the Civil War, Portland continued its growth. The era of steamships had arrived, shipbuilding tonnage had increased greatly, and the shipping industry was at its peak, as over two hundred sailing vessels called the waterfront home. The population had risen to over twenty-six thousand, and it was very difficult to find a place to live. One local newspaper, the *Eastern Argus,* reported in its September 19, 1854, edition, "We learn that the demand for houses is much greater than the supply, and some of our citizens who have been engaged in the uncomfortable business of 'house hunting' for several months tell us they must move out of the city or lodge in the street."

Two important personages visited Portland in 1860. In August, during the presidential campaign, the Democratic candidate, Stephen A. Douglas, came as part of a whistle-stop trip from Bangor to Boston. He spoke at the railroad station and then participated in a parade up Congress Street to the Preble House, where he spoke again, urging the federal government to stay out of the slavery question. Two months later, on October 20, Portland received a royal visitor when the Prince of Wales, on a tour of this country, made a short visit to the city; his ship, the HMS *Hero,* was anchored in the harbor ready to take him back to England. The future King Edward VII had traveled from New York in a special three-car train, saluted by welcoming cannon fire along the way. The train rolled slowly along Commercial Street to its destination, the Grand Trunk terminal, passing crowds jammed alongside the tracks. Flags were flying everywhere and companies of militia served as a guard and escort.

When the prince left the train, he boarded a beautiful carriage drawn by four matched bay horses. As a band played "God Save the Queen," the entourage left the depot and made its way up India Street to Congress

# Joshua Lawrence Chamberlain

OCCUPATION: Educator, soldier

LIFETIME: 1828–1914

FAMILY: Born to Joshua and Sarah Chamberlain in Brewer, Maine. Married Frances Adams, two children, Grace and Harold.

ACCOMPLISHMENTS: Graduated from Bowdoin College and Bangor Theological Seminary; began teaching at Bowdoin in 1855. Later served as president of the college for twelve years. In 1862 he joined the 20th Maine Infantry Regiment as a lieutenant colonel and gained fame and the Medal of Honor at the battle of Little Round Top at Gettysburg on July 2, 1863. Wounded six times during the Civil War and reached the rank of major general. Chosen by General Grant to receive the Confederate surrender at Appomattox Courthouse at war's end. Served four terms as governor of Maine. Although he lived in Brunswick, Maine, most of his life, he spent the last fourteen years living and working in Portland.

GREATEST CHALLENGE: Seriously injured with what was considered a mortal wound at Petersburg in 1864, he managed to survive but suffered great pain the rest of his life.

Joshua Lawrence Chamberlain

*"My darling wife, I am lying mortally wounded the doctors think, but my mind & heart are at peace. Jesus Christ is my all-sufficient savior. I go to him. God bless & keep & comfort you, precious one, you have been a precious wife to me."*

# Nathaniel Gordon

OCCUPATION: Sea captain

LIFETIME: ca. 1834–1862

FAMILY: Wife and one son.

ACCOMPLISHMENTS: Born in Portland, Gordon went on to become one of the most success-ful persons—and one of the most infamous—involved in the slave trade, which had been legally declared an act of piracy with the passage of an 1820 law. In 1860 Gordon's ship, carrying 897 slaves, was captured near the loading point in Africa by a U.S. Navy ship. At his trial in New York City, he was convicted and sentenced to death by hanging, the first slave trader to suffer such a fate.

GREATEST CHALLENGE: After Lincoln refused to commute his death sentence, scheduled for February 21, 1862, Gordon unsuc-cessfully attempted suicide by poisoning himself a few hours before the appointed time. He was resuscitated and shortly thereafter was walked to the gallows and his death.

Nathaniel Gordon

*"Well, a man can't die but once; I'm not afraid."*

Street and then to High Street. The streets were lined with flag-waving, cheering spectators whose efforts were rewarded by a tip of the princely hat and a bow. When the procession finally made its way to its final destination, the Victoria wharves at the Eastern Promenade, there was another huge crowd waiting. The prince had arrived in Portland at 1:40 P.M., and just four hours and ten minutes later, the *Hero*'s anchor was raised, and he was on his way back to England.

Something else came to Portland that was not quite as welcome, and that was Prohibition. In 1851, capitalizing on its reputation ("as Maine goes, so goes the nation"), Maine passed the first temperance law in the country, owing largely to the work and influence of Portland's mayor, Neal Dow, president of the Maine Temperance Union.

McGlinchey's Brewery on Fore Street on Munjoy Hill was known as "the last building used as a brewery in Maine." Prohibition in the state put an end to legal drinking for many years to come.

The law required a license to sell intoxicating liquor and then only for so-called medicinal purposes. A provision for search and seizure was included, and it took only three voters who suspected any illegal sales in commercial buildings to obtain a search warrant. Despite the attempts of many over the years to rid the state of the law by referenda, the voters always turned away these attempts. Abuses of the law were many and even with Prohibition, sale of liquor became a five-million-dollar-a-year business. (The country would not follow Maine's path until 1920, when Congress passed the Eighteenth Amendment, a measure that lasted for a far shorter time than Maine's law, only thirteen years; it was repealed in 1933.)

The questions of Southern rights and slavery were tearing the nation apart in the mid-nineteenth century, and the election of Lincoln in 1860 finally completed the split. On April 12, 1861, America entered one of its darkest periods when Fort Sumter, in the harbor of Charleston, South Carolina, was bombarded by Southern forces, thus precipitating the start of the Civil War. Like those in the rest of the country, Portland residents were divided over the abolition of slavery. Nevertheless, the city became a stop on the Underground Railroad, helping to move escaped slaves to safety.

Portland as a whole grew during the war because of the high demand for supplies, and business and industry continued to grow. But it suffered losses also, especially in the shipping industry, as Confederate privateers did their best to destroy or capture Northern ships and their cargoes. Other than the 3,636 men Portland contributed to the army and navy, more than 10 percent of its population, the city saw little battle action, at least until June 26, 1863.

Portland Harbor as seen from Munjoy Hill, ca. 1850. This view, painted by Charles Beckett, shows Martin's Point, formerly the site of the Marine Hospital, Grand Trunk Bridge, and the Veranda Hotel. Today the land jutting out into the water is the home of a private medical group.

On that fateful day, a Confederate privateer captained by a Lieutenant Reed entered Casco Bay, where he captured a fishing schooner called the *Archer.* Abandoning and destroying his own ship, he then sailed the *Archer* into Portland Harbor in the evening and anchored off Fish Point. His mission was to capture the revenue cutter *Caleb Cushing,* also anchored in the harbor, and set fire to Portland's wharves and the other ships. Lieutenant Reed and his men boarded the *Cushing* and captured the crew, but their luck changed when the wind died suddenly, forcing the Confederates to use the *Archer* to tow their prize out to sea.

The entire event was watched from the top of the Portland Observatory on Munjoy Hill, and word of the attack spread quickly. Fearing the arrival of a Confederate fleet, residents appropriated some local steamers and furnished them with arms and ordnance. Manned by volunteers, the steamers quickly sailed in pursuit of the *Archer.*

The *Caleb Cushing,* a sailing vessel and thus hampered by the lack of wind, had no chance of escaping the much faster steamboats. The raiders also mistakenly identified one of the pursuing steamers as a gunboat and, unwilling to give their prize back, set the *Cushing* on fire. They managed to abandon it just before the flames reached the powder magazine, and a huge explosion sent the *Caleb Cushing* to the bottom. The rebel crew was taken prisoner and hauled back to Portland, where they were tossed in jail.

Besides the inevitable loss of lives in the battles of the Civil War, Portland suffered great and permanent injury from the overall damage the

# Thomas Brackett Reed

OCCUPATION: Lawyer, politician

LIFETIME: 1839–1902

ACCOMPLISHMENTS: Graduated from Bowdoin College in 1860. Studied law and was admitted to the bar in 1865 after acting as assistant paymaster, U.S. Navy, during the last year of the Civil War. Practiced in Portland and served in the Maine House and Senate and as attorney general and Portland city solicitor. Elected to Congress in 1877 and served eleven terms; was Speaker of the House of Representatives in the Fifty-first, Fifty-fourth, and Fifty-fifth Congresses. His social circle included intellectuals and politicians from Theodore Roosevelt to Mark Twain. In his early days in Washington, he was often mistaken for President Grover Cleveland because of his height and girth. He was unsuccessful in his attempt to gain the 1896 Republican presidential nomination and resigned from Congress in 1900.

GREATEST CONTROVERSY: Reed's successful attempt to streamline the House resulted in heated backroom infighting that was at times threatening. His cunning and technical skill ultimately won out.

Thomas Brackett Reed

*"The best system is to have one party govern and the other party watch."*

Confederate privateers inflicted on its commerce as they swept its ships from the sea. After the war ended, in April 1865, strict new navigation laws went into effect that led to the transferring of most of the oceangoing business to foreign ships, thereby eliminating the business that had made the port of Portland preeminent.

At the close of the Civil War, business in Portland was still active despite the heavy debt incurred by the war itself. Street railways played a large part in

ABOVE: A painting by George F. Morse shows the Great Fire of 1866 from the Eastern Cemetery. More than 1,500 buildings were destroyed and 10,000 people left homeless.

BELOW: Edward F. Smith portrayed Portland in 1866, shortly before the Great Fire. The population was 28,500.

the city's growth. Horse-drawn street-cars began rolling over tracks in 1863, when the Portland Railroad Company began operating to allow citizens access to various parts of their city.

Middle Street was the main avenue and thoroughfare, considered by many a particularly handsome street. It was the site of most wholesale, retail, and commercial business, lined by two- and three-story buildings constructed largely of brick and stone. Offices, banks, brokerage houses, and auction rooms were principally to be found in brick buildings on Exchange Street, while Congress Street was the home of City Hall, public buildings, and churches, as well as some manufacturing companies. The residential section lay west of Monument Square.

A year after the end of the Civil War, Portland's prospects for the future seemed bright, and when July 4, 1866, rolled around, city residents were ready to celebrate the holiday in a special way. Public and private buildings were patriotically decorated with flags and bunting. The air was filled with the sounds of ringing bells and cannon fire, and a long parade of military companies, firemen, members of civic organizations, and floats made its way through the streets. A traveling circus visiting the area set up its big tent in the Deering pasture, just west of High Street.

About four o'clock in the afternoon, the merrymaking was suddenly interrupted by the sound of a ringing firebell, its alarm carried over the city by the howling of a strong southerly wind that has suddenly sprung up. Some unknown person had apparently been setting off firecrackers close to a boatbuilder's shop on Commercial Street, and it wasn't long before wood shavings in front of the building burst into flames. Fore Street, directly behind the shop, was lined with wooden buildings, and on the other side of nearby Maple Street stood Brown's large sugar factory.

After Portland's Great Fire on July 4, 1866, much of the city lay in ruins. This stereoscopic view of the destruction, looking down Middle Street, shows portions of Temple and Exchange Streets.

The strong wind quickly spread the flames to the Fore Street houses, and blazing debris was blown to Brown's building, which was full of combustible materials. The conflagration soon became uncontrollable, rapidly exhausting the meager water supply from reservoirs, cisterns, and wells and making the job of the underequipped and understaffed fire department impossible. As they pushed the advancing fire rapidly eastward, the high winds were strengthened to nearly hurricane force by the draft created by the heat, and the air was filled with blazing materials that soon covered the streets and landed on dry shingled roofs.

According to the July 6 edition of the *Portland Daily Advertiser,* "The fire raced through the city from the foot of High Street to North Street on Munjoy Hill, destroying everything in its tracks so completely that the lines of the streets can hardly be traced, and a space 1½ miles long by a quarter of a mile wide appears like a forest of chimneys with fragments of walls attached to them." The paper went on: "It is estimated that 1500 buildings have been destroyed. The loss is estimated, roughly, at fifteen million of dollars. So far as we have been able to learn there is insurance for upwards of $4,000,000."

It made no difference what the buildings were made of, as the conflagration destroyed everything from wood to brick to stone, all unable to stand up to the intense heat and flames. The heat was so fierce that the streetcar tracks in the center of Middle Street were twisted and bent out of shape. The fire raged through the night, stopping only when there was nothing left to burn. It had raged on a diagonal line from Commercial Street to Back Cove and up Munjoy Hill, roughly the same area destroyed by Captain Mowatt and the British fleet in 1775. Somehow the Portland Observatory escaped damage, and from it the view was a landscape of utter destruction.

A tent city provides shelter for many burned-out Portland residents after the 1866 fire.

John Bundy Brown was one of the heaviest losers financially; his loss was estimated at one million dollars, 60 percent of which was covered by insurance.

The Great Fire was indiscriminate in its rage; it destroyed eight churches, eight hotels, every newspaper office, all the banks, and every lawyer's office in the city. Many homeowners, fearful of the oncoming fire, had hastily moved their furniture and personal belongings to what they considered safe areas, only to discover that they weren't safe at all.

Much of the blame was attributed to the city in its unpreparedness for such a calamity and its lack of an adequate water supply. The *Portland Advertiser* proclaimed: "The great desideratum was water. The wells and cisterns were drained early. Water, water, was the universal cry. The firemen on account of their almost superhuman exertions were paralyzed. And yet the wall of fire walked on—no check anywhere: PORTLAND WAS DOOMED!"

The lack of sufficient water led to the formation in 1867 of the Portland Water Company, whose mission was to bring water from Sebago Lake; by July 4, 1870, water finally began flowing into the city.

The Great Fire of 1866, the largest and most destructive ever seen in the United States to that time, made headlines in newspapers across the country. *Harper's Weekly* devoted its entire front page to sketches of the damage.

In the fire's aftermath, the foremost question was how to provide food and shelter to the thousands left homeless and destitute, and a relief committee was quickly organized. Huge pots were built to cook food for the needy. Munjoy Hill became a tent city for the homeless, and barracks were built in unburned areas. Generous contributions of money and supplies were received from all over the country, and, fortunately, the weather remained favorable. The city survived.

Rebuilding Portland began almost immediately. The fire loss was so great, however, that most of the local insurance companies were unable to meet their obligations. Despite the severe losses and financial burden, reconstruction progressed and Portland grew into a more modern and more beautiful city.

# 6 portland rises from the ashes

Nothing that is shall perish utterly,
but perish only to revive again
In other forms, as clouds restore in rain
The exhalations of the land and sea.

—*Henry Wadsworth Longfellow, "Michael Angelo: Dedication"*

AFTER THE GREAT FIRE, which Longfellow described following a visit to his hometown as "desolation! It reminds me of Pompeii," a period of modernization and expansion began to change the face of Portland.

Many of the new buildings were constructed of brick—as a fireproofing measure—and the city began to

develop more public spaces and expand beyond the peninsula. Communications became easier as telephone service was introduced in Portland in 1878. A year later Nathaniel and Henry Deering donated a forty-acre tract of land, now known as Deering's Oaks, to the city for tax concessions to their adjoining property. Electricity began to light Portland homes in 1883, and a short time later it would be used to power the new electric streetcars that replaced the horse-drawn cars.

To ensure an adequate supply of water in case of future emergencies, reservoirs were built on Munjoy and Bramhall Hills. The Munjoy Hill reservoir gave way in 1893, causing serious damage when its 20 million gallons of water cascaded down the promenade. Automobiles finally drove into Portland in 1899; the same year the town of Deering, after the state legislature gave its approval, was annexed and became part of Portland.

There were other changes after the fire that improved conditions for residents. A two-and-a-half-acre section of land closely covered with older, smaller buildings was condemned and turned into Phoenix Park (later called Lincoln Park), a firebreak between the old and newly rebuilt sections. Portland added another park with the acquisition of Fort Allen Park on the Eastern Promenade. A new City Hall was built on Congress Street at the head of Exchange Street, replacing the old City

A Charles Goodhue sketch of Fort Allen, as it appeared in 1845. The location, now known as Fort Allen Park, provides a scenic view of Portland Harbor.

Hall, which had burned in the fire. The Maine General Hospital, now the Maine Medical Center, was also constructed, and the public library was expanded.

Two new monuments were erected to improve Portland's landscape, one to Henry Wadsworth Longfellow in 1888 in the renamed Longfellow Square, the other the Soldiers and Sailors Monument honoring the fallen heroes of the Civil War, in Monument Square, in 1891.

What once had been nearly impassable city streets and country roads were improved by the addition of strong and serviceable cobblestone pavement. Examples of these rough surfaces have been preserved and still thump under the wheels of today's cars.

Portland gained national attention in 1885 when the country's Civil War veterans gathered there for the Nineteenth National Encampment of the veterans' group the Grand Army of the Republic. Munjoy Hill was again turned into a giant tent city for the attendees and named Camp U. S. Grant. Large parades snaked through the streets, and the old soldiers were entertained by many social events held in their honor.

On November 17, 1898, Portland residents woke up to shocking news in the local newspaper. Two weather disturbances had collided during the night, causing heavy snow and extremely high winds that resulted in the sinking of the Portland-to-Boston steamship, the SS *Portland*. All of the nearly two

# Holman S. Melcher

OCCUPATION: Businessman, soldier

LIFETIME: 1841–1905

FAMILY: Married Alice Hart, one daughter.

ACCOMPLISHMENTS: Attended Bates College until the outbreak of the Civil War, when he enlisted in the famed 20th Maine Infantry Regiment in 1862. Rising in rank from corporal to major, he fought alongside Joshua Chamberlain at the Battle of Gettysburg. He was badly wounded in the Battle of Spotsylvania but survived the war. He went on to become a successful wholesale grocer in Portland and was elected to two terms as mayor of the city.

GREATEST CONTROVERSY: Melcher asserted in his published writings that it was he, and not Joshua Lawrence Chamberlain, who was responsible for initiating the famous bayonet charge down Little Round Top at Gettysburg, which helped to rescue the Union forces from defeat.

Holman S. Melcher

hundred passengers and crew aboard were lost. The hardest hit was the local African American community, which had supplied many of the sixty-five crewmen. The Abyssinian Church's congregation was terribly hard hit, losing two trustees and seventeen other members. According to the historian Herb Adams, "The blow was so heavy that it quite literally wiped out the active supporters . . . and within 12 years the congregation was down to about seven active members."

An official court investigation of the tragic sinking resulted in the verdict that the ship was lost through an act of God, although many thought the captain, Hollis Blanchard, was responsible. He had been warned by his company of the impending conditions and was told it would be best if the ship stayed at its dock. He ignored the warning and left for Portland, only to face ninety-mile-an-hour winds and seas running over thirty feet high and ultimate disaster.

The nineteenth century ended as the country faced another war, this one precipitated by the blowing up of the battleship *Maine* in Havana Harbor. Only one Maine man was serving aboard the ship, a Portland native, J. M. Doulott. Luckily, he was on shore leave when the explosion ripped through the battleship, killing 258 of the 350-man crew.

Portland's contribution to the Spanish-American War was to provide 25 percent of the

ABOVE: The coastal steamer *Portland* under way to its destination in Boston. The ship sank during a ferocious storm in 1898, killing all on board.

BELOW: The battleship *Maine* was sunk in Havana Harbor in 1898, which sparked the Spanish-American War. One of the ship's big guns was recovered and now rests at Fort Allen Park.

companies of the First Maine Regiment. During the short war, two ships were sent out to patrol Maine's waters. Lighthouses were darkened, Fort Preble was manned, harbors and rivers were mined, and the *Montauk,* a Civil War monitor-class ship crewed by 125 Portland Naval Reservists, protected the city.

In the twenty-year period following the turn of the twentieth century, Portland residents' lives were changed forever when the automobile chugged into town. It was on July 19, 1899, that the photographer Maynard D. Hanson took delivery of the city's first car, a steam-powered Locomobil. As Hanson puffed his way up Congress Street, he was greeted by a large crowd eager to view the new spectacle.

The speed limit on Portland's streets was a fast eight miles an hour, and gas cost about fourteen cents a gallon. Cars were priced between one and two thousand dollars, and a family needed an annual income of at least two thousand dollars to be able to afford a new car. In spite of the cost, ownership grew rapidly, and by 1920 Portland and the state had been transformed by the car and truck.

James P. Baxter (1831–1921), a wealthy manufacturer and former mayor of Portland, devoted his life to the general betterment of Portland. He gave the city its first public library and played a great part in creating the city's park system.

In 1908 Portland lost its second City Hall, located on Congress Street, when a fire broke out in the electrical system on January 24. The blaze spread rapidly through the building, causing $600,000 in damages, only $80,000 of which was covered by insurance. City officials favored a plan to rebuild City Hall at a new location, the eastern end of Lincoln Park. Voters turned down the plan in a referendum and chose to keep City Hall where it had stood on Congress Street. Three years later, in 1912, the new building was dedicated. Over the front door is the city's motto in wrought iron, *Resurgam,* Latin for "I shall rise again."

At the turn of the century Portland's population had grown to over fifty thousand, and as modernization and expansion continued, so did this growth in the number of inhabitants. In the next twenty years, the population grew to nearly seventy thousand, which created a demand for bigger and better things. A new Cumberland County Courthouse and Federal Customs House were built to handle government business, and in 1915 social activities were taken care of with the construction of the Portland Exposition Building.

Spring Point Light in Portland Harbor, ca. 1900. The lighthouse is now connected to the shore by a granite causeway.

# *Cyrus Hermann Kotzschmar Curtis*

OCCUPATION: Publisher

LIFETIME: 1850–1933

FAMILY: Son of Cyrus Libby Curtis.

ACCOMPLISHMENTS:
Born in Portland but moved to Philadelphia at the age of sixteen. Established a journalistic empire there and played a significant part in modern magazine publishing. Founded the Curtis Publishing Company; his publications included *Ladies Home Journal* and the *Saturday Evening Post*. Known for his philanthropy to hospitals, museums, and schools. He gave the City of Portland a grand Austin organ in memory of a family friend, Hermann Kotzschmar, that today is a mainstay at the city's Merrill Auditorium.

Cyrus Hermann Kotzschmar Curtis

Entertainment was provided by a number of theaters that featured the very popular vaudeville shows that were touring the country showcasing famous performers. A new form of entertainment was becoming popular, however, which began drawing patrons away from the live shows; this was the newest innovation, the flickering action flashed on the silver screen. By the 1930s Portland had ten theaters, but only two offered live shows. Movies finally took over completely when the last legitimate theater, the Jefferson, a 1,600-seat facility that had opened in 1896, closed its doors in 1933 and ended an era.

Even the Portland Railroad Company wanted a piece of the entertainment action. With its tracks now stretching across Portland, the company built Riverton Park in an attempt to increase passengers. It was a lavish

Portland City Hall was destroyed by an electrical fire on January 24, 1908. The blaze also destroyed many Cumberland County records. A new City Hall was built on the footprint of the old and opened in 1912.

undertaking, ultimately offering the public the 2,500-seat Rustic Theater, an outdoor entertainment venue, as well as pavilions for picnicking and canoes for rowing. The Casco Bay islands also took part in the theatrical rush when the Gem Theater opened on Peaks Island in 1898. Initially built as a roller-skating rink, it was converted to a 1,500-seat theater with adjoining refreshment rooms.

Two big projects were completed just before the beginning of World War I. Baxter Boulevard, winding through Back Cove between the water and the newly built Payson Park, was completed, and a new bridge spanned the Fore River, connecting Portland with South Portland. Opening to traffic on July 20, 1916, the new bridge was aptly named the "million-dollar bridge" because of its cost. It replaced an ancient, wooden, hand-operated drawbridge built in 1822 that was, over the years, the scene of many accidents, especially at the Portland end. Today travelers cross the Fore River on the new Casco Bay Bridge, completed at the beginning of the twenty-first century.

The Jefferson Theater, built in 1897, stood at the corner of Free and Oak Streets. It provided entertainment until it was torn down in 1933.

Entrance to Riverton Park, ca. 1895. Built by the trolley company to increase ridership, the park provided a large entertainment venue for Portland residents.

On April 16, 1917, the United States declared war on Germany, finally entering the "war to end all wars" after a period of isolationism. Maine contributed heavily financially and with manpower, much of it coming from Portland. The Second Maine Infantry was federalized on April 26, and two companies were moved to Portland to undergo the thorough training demanded by General John J. Pershing, the American commander.

Congress put out a call for volunteers and instituted a draft. Portland satisfied its obligation entirely with volunteers. Once Maine became involved in the actual fighting, the wounded began flowing through Portland. The city's residents gradually discarded their life-as-usual attitude to make an all-out effort of support. Enlistments grew, money was raised for the war effort, and shortages of food and fuel were endured. War bonds and savings stamps were bought by both young and old. Even grocery shopping was affected because of a shortage of farm-workers and the government's curtailing of the use of certain products. When the armistice ending the war was signed on November 11, 1918, the troops came home in large numbers. The first American Legion post was organized and named the Harold T. Andrews Post in honor of the first Portland soldier to die in the Great War.

The 1920s were glittering and exciting years that slowly descended into hard times and the Depression. In the early twenties there was a commercial building boom in Portland. The Maine State Pier, at the eastern end of Commercial Street, was dedicated on September 13, 1923. The thousand-foot-long structure was to benefit the entire state by allowing products from all over to be shipped to a waiting world. The following year, on the site of the Preble House at Monument Square, which had been a major hotel for fifty years, the twelve-story Chapman Building went up, the tallest structure in the state. It contained forty stores, many offices, and the Chapman National Bank. The most unusual feature was an arcade that ran from Congress Street to the Preble Street entrance of Keith's Theater. The walkway was lined with shops on both sides and can be viewed as a precursor to today's malls.

# Percival P. Baxter

OCCUPATION: Businessman, politician

LIFETIME: 1876–1969

FAMILY: Born in Portland, the son of James Phinney Baxter and one of eight children, he remained a lifelong bachelor.

ACCOMPLISHMENTS: Graduated from Harvard Law School and admitted to the bar but never practiced for a livelihood. Inherited not only his father's wealth but also his outdoor interests and philanthropic ideals. Developed a great passion for making Mt. Katahdin and the surrounding wilderness a park and worked the for rest of his life to achieve that aim. During his four years as governor he urged the legislature to acquire the mountain as a park but could not persuade it to do so. He spent the next thirty-three years privately purchasing the land and giving it to the state. It was named Baxter State Park in his honor.

GREATEST CHALLENGE: Fending off state and federal political challenges to turn his gift into a national park, Baxter carefully crafted deeds of trust that controlled the lands over the years.

Percival P. Baxter

On September 10, 1923, Portland's government changed from a mayor–common council government to a manager–council administration. The change was preceded by much nasty infighting, primarily because of the large part played by the Ku Klux Klan, which sought to dominate local and state politics in many states, including Maine. Its headquarters in Portland was a large complex of buildings on Forest Avenue. Three days before the election, the Klan held two rallies in the City Hall auditorium, which drew a crowd of nearly six thousand to hear their pro-change argu-

Map of Portland, 1928.

ments. There was also a pro change lobby whose arguments dealt directly with religion. The anti-change contingent claimed the Klan and its supporters were agents of the Protestant community and anti-Catholic. Even Portland's two competing newspapers, the *Press Herald* and the *Evening Express,* took opposite sides, making no attempt to balance their news coverage. The pro-change slate of candidates was swept into office, forming an all-Protestant City Council.

Portland's role as the winter port for Montreal was greatly diminished when the Canadian government, in a surge of nationalism, decided to subsidize its own ports, which slowly decreased the amount of grain tonnage shipped to Portland. The Grand Trunk Railroad was also absorbed into the government-owned Canadian National Railway. The changes came despite the fact that the distance from Montreal to Halifax was 800 miles, 600 to St. Johns, and only 297 to Portland. Extra locomotives were needed for the maritime run. Millions of Canadian dollars were spent developing new Canadian waterfront facilities, and freight rates were much higher. Nevertheless, nationalism prevailed, and Portland lost its lucrative role as Canada's winter port.

The years between 1929 and 1941 were terrible years for Portland and the rest of

The Eastland Hotel on High Street under construction in 1927. It was attached to the Congress Square Hotel. Both buildings were owned by the Rines family.

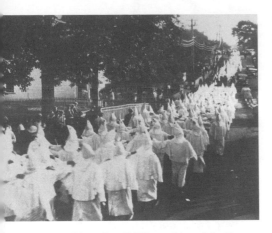

More than 7,000 members of the Ku Klux Klan gathered in Portland in 1923 in a successful attempt to change the form of the city's government. The Klan had a huge headquarters complex on Forest Avenue.

the country. In October 1929 the stock market crashed, sending the world into a deep depression. In the early 1930s unemployment ran as high as 25 percent. Prices dropped about 25 percent, but the money supply slipped by 35 percent. In 1933 the banks failed. Wages held steady or declined and jobs became scarcer. Many employees, lucky to have a job, were forced to accept pay cuts just to keep their jobs. Apartments were plentiful, the rents cheap, and a new five-room house sold for as little as three thousand dollars.

During the Great Depression, the administration of Franklin Roosevelt created a multitude of assistance agencies, bureaus, and authorities. The most important of these was the WPA, the Works Project Administration. It replaced a direct dole system that gave money to the jobless by providing them work instead at salaries ranging from fifteen to ninety dollars a month. One of the projects was the building in 1939 of the state's first traffic circle at St. John and Danforth Streets in Portland. Building things was not the only activity of the WPA. There were many underagencies, such as the Federal Writers Project and the Federal Arts Project, which put the city's writers and artists to work.

The Depression lingered until 1941, when the United States declared war on Germany and Japan after the bombing of Pearl Harbor. Portland's future took a definite upswing when this country decided to help war-torn Britain, which was in desperate

President Theodore Roosevelt waves his hat to the crowd gathered outside the home of Thomas B. Reed during a 1902 visit to the city.

## John Ford

OCCUPATION: Movie director

LIFETIME: 1894–1973

FAMILY: Wife, Mary, and one son and one daughter.

ACCOMPLISHMENTS: Born John Martin Feeney in Cape Elizabeth, Maine, but raised in Portland, he followed one of his brothers, an actor, to Hollywood. When asked what brought him to Hollywood, he replied, "The train." He was one of the most accomplished film directors for over thirty years, and he won four directing Oscars, more that any other director. He also won two Oscars for documentaries filmed during World War II, when he served on active duty, reaching the rank of rear admiral. He received a Presidential Medal of Freedom from Richard Nixon. Ford's films and style of film-making have influenced such directors as Martin Scorsese, Steven Spielberg, and Sam Peckinpah, as well as countless others.

John Ford

need of replacing cargo ships that were being sunk at an alarming rate by German submarines.

In December 1940, a year before the United States entered the war, the Todd-Bath Iron Shipbuilding Corporation contracted to build thirty ocean-class ships for England. Cushing Point, a community of small houses in South Portland, was chosen as the site of a new seven-basin shipyard to build these ships. The area was the scene of massive activity as workers

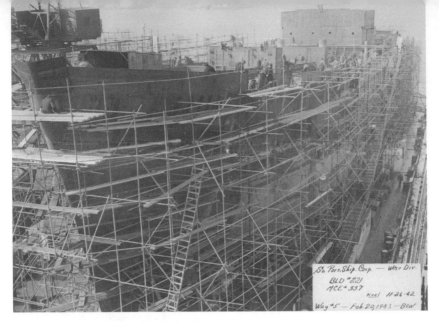

The bow of a Liberty ship rests on way no. 5 at the South Portland Shipbuilding Corporation in 1943. The company was a major builder for the navy during World War II and provided employment for over 30,000 workers.

rushed to complete the yard before work on the first ship was due to begin. Called the East Yard, it took only five months from groundbreaking to the laying of the first keel.

Meanwhile, as the East Yard was being readied, the U.S. Maritime Commission began realizing the sad state of American shipping and, even though the country was not technically at war, ordered the building of more new shipyards. Todd-Bath won a contract for one of the new yards and built it on the western side of Cushing Point, calling it the South Portland Shipbuilding Corporation. The new site, a conventional six-way facility, faced Portland across the harbor and was designated the West Yard. As the shipyards were completed, thousands of workers flocked to the area to take advantage of the three-shift, seven-day-a-week schedule. Training was offered in many fields to those who were inexperienced in the methods of building Liberty ships.

In his 1945 history of the yards, *Portland Ships Are Good Ships,* Herbert G. Jones wrote, "An organization of nearly thirty thousand shipbuilders was created almost overnight. A migratory army of unskilled help flocked to the yard from every community in the state of Maine as well as from neighboring states. Scarcity of materials, lack of suitable yard machinery, and the necessity of training green hands called for superhuman effort on the part of both labor and management alike." Women were hired and trained for a variety of jobs, from machine workers to crane operators. As many as 3,700 women aided the war effort by building ships. By war's end, a total of 266 ships had been launched to aid the war effort.

July 1941 saw the laying of the first mile of pipe to transport oil from Portland to Montreal. The 297-mile pipeline was built because the severe shortage of tankers had cut the flow of oil by about 200,000 barrels daily.

Founded in 1865, the Russell Shipbuilding Company at Kensington and Berwick Streets built wooden ships for use in World War I. This 1919 painting by Krouthen shows two hulls under construction.

The U.S. Navy began to make its presence known in the Portland area at the beginning of 1941. Residents noticed an increasing number of sailors on the streets, and camouflaged warships were showing up in the harbor with greater frequency. Casco Bay had become the navy's official anchorage for its North Atlantic Fleet, a major naval operation. The islands also played their part. Peaks Island became a military reservation, Long Island held the Naval Fuel Depot, and Little Chebeague Island was the Naval Recreation Center. The ocean sides of the islands were filled with minefields, underwater detection devices, and submarine nets.

There were many discomforts and annoyances that plagued Greater Portland citizens during the war. The crush of civilian workers and military personnel created a great shortage of housing. It was almost impossible to find a place to live, and in Portland and surrounding areas, whole villages of emergency houses sprung up. Thousands of workers unable to find housing nearby were forced to take shipyard buses from outlying areas.

Portland's importance militarily during the war created fear that an enemy attack would take place. The skyline became a homing beacon for German submarines, and rumbling in the skies spooked many people. Aircraft spotters, air-raid wardens, and auxiliary police were everywhere, while test blackouts and air-raid drills kept people on their toes.

When peace finally came on August 14, 1945, Greater Portland celebrated in a huge way. As the news of peace spread, crowds swarmed Monument Square and Congress Street, growing to nearly one hundred thousand cheering people.

# 7

## back to the future

Strange to me now are the forms I meet
When I visit the dear old town;
But the native air is pure and sweet,
And the trees that o'ershadow each well-known street
As they balance up and down.

—*Henry Wadsworth Longfellow, "My Lost Youth"*

THE YEARS FOLLOWING World War II saw the direction of Portland's fortunes take a slow downward turn. The great flow of money coming into the city during the war slowed to a trickle. Defense-related jobs were gone, and much of the temporary housing that had been put up was in deplorable condition. The population that had

An aerial view of Portland's West End, ca. 1950, showing Union Station at the lower left and Maine General Hospital and the Bramhall-Vaughan Street Reservoir at center right.

grown because of the availability of jobs found those jobs gone, and urban decay became a major problem. People began to leave the city to look for work elsewhere. Portland's population reached its peak in 1950, when it grew to more than 77,000, but that number would drop 20 percent by 1980.

Postwar depression was not the only cause of the outflow of residents. One of the major reasons was a changing lifestyle. People didn't mind driving to get to the suburbs and nearby bedroom communities. In 1947 the Maine Turnpike, the nation's second-oldest toll road, opened from Portland to Kittery, making travel easier.

South Portland, Westbrook, Falmouth, and Cape Elizabeth all experienced population gains, although Portland remained the hub of the area. The growth rate of Cumberland County nevertheless slowed as job opportunities in the rest of New England attracted young people.

In 1952 the Portland City Council created the Slum Clearance and Redevelopment Authority. Its first move was to flatten a nine-block area between Middle and Fore Streets, but numerous legal challenges would delay the project for four years. When work finally began, entire blocks were knocked down, including both good and bad. The area, called Vine-Deer-Chatham, had been home to sixty-two families. Many of the residents were Italian American and had lived there since their families had migrated from Italy many years earlier.

Urban renewal replaced total clearance, and rehabilitation upgraded neighborhoods in the Bayside and Munjoy Hill areas. Conservation moved

# *Elizabeth Noyce*

OCCUPATION: Philanthropist

LIFETIME: 1930–1996

FAMILY: Born Auburn, Massachusetts, to Helen and Frank Bottomley. Married to Robert Noyce, the founder of Intel; three daughters and one son.

ACCOMPLISHMENTS: Became a great influence in the redevelopment of downtown Portland after her divorce in 1975 and subsequent acquisition of great wealth. Through her foundation, the Libra Foundation, much downtown property was purchased and the Portland Public Market built. She was deeply devoted to Maine and Portland. Her generosity touched and enriched almost every aspect of the city's and state's society; she contributed millions of dollars to the Barbara Bush Children's Hospital at the Maine Medical Center and the Cumberland County Civic Center, to name but two examples.

GREATEST CHALLENGE: Providing energy and leadership to give the city and the state pride of place and hope for a better future.

Elizabeth Noyce

*"To be given a fortune and accept it not as a stroke of luck but a mission represents a kind of moral fiber that is extraordinary."—Owen Wells, attorney for Elizabeth Noyce.*

to the West End, where city improvements and low-cost loans were used to bring homes up to code.

Many displaced families had great difficulty finding decent housing, and a battle developed over whether private housing or public housing would solve the problem. City Council members were divided, and it took approval by voters to finally authorize public housing.

As Portland's old-line political machine began to lose favor, it was replaced by a younger element that began to raise the city up from the

Veterans Bridge, connecting Portland's West End on Vaughan Street with South Portland, is shown under construction in 1953.

depths it had fallen to. The 1960s began with a period of planning and more planning, but when a young local, John Menario, was hired as city manager, things really began to happen. Four new parking garages were built in the downtown area. Congress Street was transformed. The first new office building in over half a century went up, and a new library was built. The airport was expanded and Congress Square rebuilt. By the early 1970s support was growing for a new county-owned arena, and, with the approval of the City Council, voters in Cumberland County authorized spending $8 million to build the Civic Center, home to the city's professional hockey team, the Portland Pirates of the American Hockey League.

Meanwhile, downtown Portland merchants were growing alarmed as shoppers were introduced to a new way to spend their money. Shopping centers were becoming the rage because of the ease of parking and the convenience offered by many stores in one central location. August 1969 saw the opening of the largest indoor mall in the state, the Maine Mall in South Portland. Many of the downtown merchants' fears became a reality when some of the large stores closed their downtown locations and moved into the mall.

Today Portland has a well-run preservation movement to protect

Portland's entry in the double-A Eastern League is the Sea Dogs, a Boston Red Sox affiliate. The team plays its home games to sold-out crowds at Hadlock Field, one of the league's finest facilities.

many of the city's fine older buildings. Portland Landmarks was founded after two events in the 1960s raised the public consciousness. The first incident was the demolition of the city's Union Station, torn down when rail passenger service ended. When the station's beautiful granite clock tower was smashed into oblivion, a large crowd witnessed the event with sadness, and the subsequent photo of its destruction has become a best-seller. The site is now home to an ugly strip mall. The second incident was the leveling of the old post office on Middle Street, a beautiful granite structure dating back to the nineteenth century. It was replaced with a parking lot.

ABOVE: Union Station on St. John Street in 1910. Opened in 1888, the station was torn down in 1960. Its demolition led to the formation of the preservation movement in Portland.

BELOW: The armory in the Old Port Section was built in 1895 for drilling the many National Guard units that were stationed there. Today the building serves as a fine hotel.

One of the greatest achievements in making Portland what it is today was the development of the Old Port area, bordered by Federal Street to the north, Commercial Street to the south, Union Street to the west, and Pearl Street to the east. Today the Old Port is a destination for locals and tourists alike, but in the 1950s and 1960s the area was largely deserted and a target for Portland's slum clearance planners. Many of the area's buildings were empty and dilapidated, and the streets were empty of people. Soon, however, artists and craftsmen began moving in, taking advantage of low rent to start their own businesses.

# Judd Asher Nelson

OCCUPATION: Actor, writer

LIFETIME: b. 1959

FAMILY: Son of Leonard and Merle Nelson; two sisters.

ACCOMPLISHMENTS: Born in Portland, Nelson began his acting career while watching a friend's audition and had to audition himself in order to stay. He got the part. Nelson was one of several actors dubbed by the media as the "Brat Pack." His films include *The Breakfast Club, St. Elmo's Fire,* and *New Jack City.* From 1996 to 1999 he appeared in the hit TV series *Suddenly Susan,* costarring with Brooke Shields. His performance list includes many roles in television and film.

Judd Asher Nelson

This group planted the seed for what was to become one of Portland's premier attractions; the Old Port Association was soon organized to protect the area from the city's plans to level many of the buildings. The Old Port began to experience economic growth and success despite the skepticism of many in the business community. At first, banks refused to loan start-up money, but gradually the general concept became accepted. Property values and taxes grew to the point where the city began to do its share in the revitalization of the Old Port. Sidewalks were built, streets repaired, and trees planted, and in the 1980s most of the rental space was filled. Today the Old Port is a very busy area with a bright future, offering something for everyone. It is a blend of old and new charm; certain sections of some streets still display the original cobblestones.

Another facet of Portland's popularity as a tourist destination is its international ferry service to Nova Scotia. Beginning in the summer of 1970 with service to Yarmouth, Nova Scotia, the seasonal daily round-trips continued until a dispute between the ferry company and the city over the safety of the terminal building caused a parting of the ways. Portland lost the service for a year until a contract was signed with the Bay Ferry Company, operators of a high-speed boat from Bar Harbor. In 2006 the company also began offering weekend service from Portland to Yarmouth, Nova Scotia.

Also serving Portland and the islands in Casco Bay are the ferries of Casco Bay Lines. They provide island residents and tourists transportation from the city to the various islands on a regular schedule and also offer short scenic cruises.

With the growth of malls and shopping centers, much of the downtown Portland business community lost its customer base. Slowly, however, the area has experienced revitalization. Many millions of dollars from government and private sources have resulted in the construction of major new office buildings. Monument Square was reconstructed, making it more shopper-friendly. New eating establishments have opened, a farmer's market is held weekly, and free entertainment is provided during the summer months. It is a lively and busy place for shoppers and office workers to gather for a break from their busy schedules.

Many of the empty stores on Congress Street, vacated when their occupants moved to the surrounding malls, became filled with new businesses, especially after L.L. Bean opened an outlet store on the main street that, like a magnet, attracted other new businesses to do the same. Travel to Portland from outlying communities was made easier when I-295 opened in 1974. Circling the city, the highway has many convenient exits that allow potential shoppers to save time and effort in reaching their destinations in Portland.

A section of Congress Street from Longfellow Square to Monument Square was designated as the Arts District, an artist-friendly area filled with studios, art galleries, and, at Congress Square, the Portland

Ferries of the Casco Bay Lines await passengers at their terminal on Commercial Street.

The McClellan-Sweat house at Spring and High Streets was built in 1801 for the shipping magnate Hugh McClellan. Restored in the 1990s, it is now part of the Portland Museum of Art and open to visitors.

Museum of Art, a world-class facility. Congress Square Park was built in 1982 to provide an area for free entertainment and as an enticement for people to visit the downtown business district.

Portland, since its earliest history, has faced many highs and lows, disasters and rebuildings, but it has always been able to raise itself to a higher level. Today it has climbed back to the top, recognized as one of the best cities in the country in many national polls. It offers something to residents and visitors alike, with a bustling arts and entertainment scene and nationally recognized eateries.

In 2006 the highly acclaimed *Frommer's Travel Guides* recognized Portland as one of the twelve must-see destinations for world travelers, noting its fantastic mix of culture and education, and its impressive number of first-rate restaurants, just one more reason for Portland residents to be proud of their city.

# chronology

## *1600s*

1632   George Cleeve and Richard Tucker settle on Falmouth Neck.
1645   Population grows to forty.
1658   Massachusetts claims jurisdiction over the Province of Maine.
1668   Eastern Cemetery is founded at the foot of Munjoy Hill.
1676   Indians attack and burn Falmouth Neck.
1680   George Bramhall buys four hundred acres at the western end of the peninsula.
1681   Fort Loyall is built at the foot of Broad (now India) Street.
1688   Growth continues as population reaches six hundred.
1689   Seven hundred Indians attack Brackett's farm (now Deering Oaks) and are
       defeated by Major Benjamin Church.
1690   Led by French army officers, Indians attack and destroy Falmouth and Fort Loyall.

## *1700s*

1700   Fort New Casco is built.
1716   Fourteen families return to Falmouth Neck, led by Major Moody.
1717   Earliest burial is recorded at Eastern Cemetery.
1718   Massachusetts General Court reincorporates Falmouth.
1719   Streets are laid out.
1727   Falmouth becomes the official mast port for England.
1739   Mast agent is appointed.
1750   First shipyard is established in Falmouth.
1775   British fleet, led by Lieutenant Henry Mowatt, bombards and destroys Falmouth.
1784   Falmouth begins rebuilding.
1786   Town of Portland is incorporated when it separates from the rest of Falmouth.
1786   General Peleg Wadsworth builds first brick house on the peninsula.
1787   Stagecoach mail and passenger service begins.
1788   New streets are laid out.
1791   Portland Head Light is lit.
1794   Fort Sumner is built.
1796   Back Cove Bridge is built.
1799   First bank is established.
1799   Vaughn's Bridge is built.

## *1800s*

1800   William Vaughn purchases four hundred acres on Bramhall Hill.
1803   James Deering buys two hundred acres of the old Brackett Farm.
1806   Portland becomes the sixth-largest port in the country.

| 1807 | Fort Preble and Fort Scammell are built. |
| 1807 | Custom House Wharf is constructed. |
| (1807) | Henry Wadsworth Longfellow is born. |
| 1807 | Lemuel Moody builds his observatory. |
| 1820 | Maine becomes a state, with Portland as its capital. |
| 1821 | Free public high school is established. |
| 1822 | Maine Historical Society is founded. |
| 1823 | Portland Bridge is built. |
| 1823 | First steamboat docks in Portland. |

*The house where the poet Henry Wadsworth Longfellow was born in 1807 on Fore Street. It was torn down in 1954. The site is marked with a small granite monument.*

| (1825) | First Parish Church is built on Congress Street to replace "Old Jerusalem." |
| 1828 | Abyssinian Church is formed by Portland's black population. |
| 1829 | Land is purchased for Western Cemetery. |
| 1829 | The daily *Portland Courier* is founded by Seba Smith. |
| 1830 | Population reaches 12,601. |
| 1830 | St. Dominic's Catholic Church is established. |
| 1830s | Portland extends streets to the Western Promenade. |
| 1831 | James Phinney Baxter is born. |
| 1831 | Portland is incorporated as a city. |
| 1832 | State capital moves from Portland to Augusta. |
| 1836 | Eastern Promenade is laid out. |
| 1842 | Railroad service to Boston begins. |
| 1845 | Brown's sugar factory is built. |
| 1847 | Portland Company is established to build locomotives. |
| 1851 | Railroad to Augusta begins operations. |
| 1851 | Commercial Street is constructed and becomes the new waterfront. |
| 1853 | Atlantic and St. Lawrence Railway to Montreal is completed. |
| 1853 | First trans-Atlantic steamship arrives. |
| 1854 | Evergreen Cemetery is consecrated. |
| 1855 | Portland is seventh in ship tonnage in United States. |
| 1856 | Bramhall Mansion construction is begun by J. B. Brown on Bramhall Hill. |
| 1857 | Secretary of War Jefferson Davis authorizes building of Fort Gorges in the harbor. |
| 1860 | Prince of Wales visits Portland. |
| 1861 | Civil War begins. |

*The First Parish Meeting House in 1720 was the first church established in Portland. It stood on the north corner of India and Middle Streets. Known as "Old Jerusalem," it was replaced in 1825 by a larger granite building.*

| 1863 | U.S. revenue cutter *Caleb Cushing* is destroyed in Portland Harbor by Confederate raiders. |
| 1863 | Portland Railroad Company begins first horse-drawn trolley service. |
| 1866 | Fire destroys much of Portland, leaving thousands homeless. |
| 1867 | Portland installs new fire alarm signal system, one of the country's first. |

*A horse-drawn trolley of the Portland Railroad Company on Congress Street, ca. 1890.*

| 1868 | Falmouth Hotel is built. |
| 1870 | Population grows to 31,413. |
| 1872 | U. S. Grant visits Portland. |
| 1872 | New Custom House is constructed. |

*The Falmouth Hotel on Middle Street was one of the finest hotels in all New England. The building is patriotically decked out for the 1872 visit of President Grant. The building was torn down in the mid-1900s.*

| 1873 | Maine General Hospital (now Maine Medical Center) opens. |
| 1878 | Telephone service arrives in Portland. |
| 1879 | Donation of Deering Oaks to the city by Nathaniel and Henry Deering is finalized. |
| 1882 | Longfellow dies in Cambridge, Mass., at the age of seventy-five. |
| 1883 | Electric power comes to Portland. |
| 1885 | Longfellow Statue Association begins raising funds for statue of the poet in Portland. |
| 1886 | Portland celebrates its centennial. |
| 1888 | Union Station is built. |
| 1888 | Longfellow's statue is dedicated in Longfellow Square. |
| 1889 | Portland Railroad Company electrifies its lines. |

*The Maine Medical Center, recognized as one of the country's safest, creates a large footprint on Portland's landscape. It is the largest medical facility in Maine and is constantly expanding to offer more services.*

1890  City acquires Fort Allen Park on the Eastern Promenade.
1890  First electric trolley service begins from Monument Square.
1891  Soldiers and Sailors Monument is dedicated in Monument Square.
1893  James Phinney Baxter is elected mayor.
1894  Jewish cemetery is established.
1896  Riverton Trolley Park is built by Portland Railroad Company.
1899  Deering is annexed by Portland and gives up its town status.

*A cannon from the War of 1812 and the mast and bridge of the heavy cruiser* Portland *from WWII are displayed at Fort Allen Park.*

## 1900s

1900  Population grows to 50,145.
1907  City Hall is destroyed by fire.
1907  First movie house opens.
1910  Statue of Thomas Brackett Reed is erected on Western Promenade.
1910  Cumberland County Courthouse is built.
1911  Federal Courthouse is built.
1912  New City Hall is completed at old location.
1915  Portland Exposition Building is built.
1915  Burnham and Morrill Company is established.

1916  New Portland Bridge opens.
1917  Payson Park is established in East Deering section.
1917  Baxter Boulevard along Back Cove is completed.
1918  Semipro Twilight Baseball League begins play.
1920  Population reaches 69,272.
1921  James Phinney Baxter dies.
1923  Air service to Portland begins.
1923  Deering High School is built.
1924  Spanish-American War Veteran's Monument is dedicated.

*The Burnham and Morrill Company, now part of a giant food conglomerate, produces B&M baked beans for nationwide distribution.*

1925  First commercial radio station, WCSH, goes on the air.
1927  Charles Lindbergh comes to Deering Oaks, where he is greeted by 25,000.
1927  Eastland Hotel opens.
1930  Portland's population swells to over 70,000.
1931  Portland Stadium is dedicated.
1932  Riverside Golf Course opens.
1933  Portland Junior College, later University of Southern Maine, opens.
1937  Ground is broken for new Portland Airport terminal.
1941  Maine Turnpike Authority is created.
1941  Shipyard opens to build Liberty ships for WWII.
1941  Trolley service ends.
1941  Portland pipeline begins delivering oil to Montreal.

| 1946 | Baxter Woods is donated to the city. |
|------|--------------------------------------|
| 1947 | First season of Portland Pilots professional baseball. |
| 1947 | Maine Turnpike from Portland to Kittery opens. |
| 1952 | Southern Maine Vocational College opens. |
| 1953 | WCSH brings first commercial television to Portland. |
| 1953 | Veterans Bridge is built. |
| 1955 | Turnpike is extended from Portland to Augusta. |
| 1959 | Pine Tree Shopping Center opens on Brighton Ave. |
| 1961 | Union Station is torn down. |
| 1964 | McDonald's raises its first arches in Portland. |
| 1966 | Grand Trunk Railroad station is demolished. |
| 1967 | Rail passenger service ends. |
| 1969 | Percival Baxter dies. |
| 1969 | Maine Mall, the largest shopping center in Maine, opens. |
| 1969 | Franklin Towers, low-income housing, is built. |
| 1970 | International ferry terminal is created. |
| 1974 | Construction of I-295 eliminates four-acre portion of Deering Oaks. |
| 1975 | Monument Square is reconstructed to make it pedestrian-friendly. |
| 1977 | Cumberland County Civic Center opens. |
| 1977 | Municipal Fish Pier is established on waterfront. |
| 1979 | Sewage treatment plant is completed at East End. |
| 1979 | New library opens. |
| 1982 | Congress Square Park is completed. |
| 1983 | New art museum opens. |
| 1989 | Walking trail around Back Cove is completed. |

## 2000s

| 2001 | Bath Iron Works facility and dry dock vacated at the end of the year. |
|------|------------------------------------------------------------------------|
| 2002 | Cianbro Corporation begins finish work on partially completed oil rigs for South American waters. The huge rigs become a dominant feature of the waterfront. |
| 2003 | First Lady Laura Bush visits Portland to highlight historic preservation. |
| 2004 | Oil-rig work is completed and the rigs are towed to South America. |
| 2005 | Groundbreaking ceremonies are held for the construction of a new cruise ship facility called Ocean Gateway. |
| 2006 | Peaks Island residents vote to break away from Portland in an unsuccessful attempt to become a town. |
| 2006 | Restoration begins on the deteriorating clock tower of Portland City Hall. |

# further reading

THE MOST VALUABLE SOURCE of Portland's history, at least until the time of the Civil War, is William Willis's *The History of Portland* (1865). It is a highly detailed source of the city's history; it includes family records of many of the most important citizens. Other valuable works include Augustus F. Moulton, *Portland by the Sea* (1926); William Willis, *Journals of the Rev. Thomas Smith, and the Rev. Samuel Deane, with Historical Notes of Portland from 1632–1849* (1849); Albert F. Barnes, editor, *Greater Portland Celebration 350* (1984); Edward H. Elwell, *Portland and Vicinity* (revised edition, 1881), Greater Portland Landmarks, *Portland* (1972), which contains an important architectural history of some of Portland's finest old houses; William Goold, *Portland in the Past; with Historical Notes of Old Falmouth* (1886); Henry E. Dunnack, *Maine Forts* (1924).

Other recent sources include Donald W. Beattie, Rodney M. Cole, and Charles G. Waugh, editors, *A Distant War Comes Home: Maine in the Civil War Era* (1996); Maine Historical Society, *The Maine Bicentennial Atlas: An Historic Survey* (1976); James S. Leamon, *Revolution Downeast: The War for American Independence in Maine* (1993); Roger F. Duncan, *Coastal Maine: A Maritime History* (1992); William David Barry, *A Vignetted History of Portland Business, 1632–1982* (1982); William David Barry with Frances W. Peabody, *Tate House, Crown of the Maine Mast Trade* (1982); Maine Historical Society, *Letters of General Peleg Wadsworth to His Son John, 1796–1798* (1961); Donald A. Yerxa, *The Burning of Falmouth, 1775: A Case Study in British Imperial Pacification* (1975); and Elizabeth Ring, *Maine in the Making of the Nation, 1783–1870* (1996).

The most current book that tells Portland's story is a collection of thirteen essays on a variety of historical subjects edited by Joseph A. Conforti, *Creating Portland: History and Place in Northern New England* (2005).

For a visual treat see Greater Portland Landmarks, *Portland: A Collection of 19th Century Engravings* (1976); and Earle G. Shettleworth Jr. and William David Barry, *Mr. Goodhue Remembers Portland: Scenes from the Mid-19th Century* (1981).

# acknowledgments

THE GENERAL CONSENSUS is that the art of writing is a solitary affair. That's only partially true. Anyone who has written a nonfiction book soon discovers that he needs a lot of help from a lot of people. *A Short History of Portland* is no exception. Without the help, expertise, and encouragement of a small army, the book would never have seen the light of day.

First, of course, is my family. I am greatly in their debt for their patience. My wife, Sandra, and my son, Michael, were helpful in reading the manuscript and offering their opinions and suggestions. My daughter, Lori, was my chief cheerleader.

I am grateful for the constant encouragement given by my Maine Historical Society colleagues. My coworker Robert Kemp kept me on the straight and narrow when I had computer problems—and there were many.

Two noted experts on Portland's history were always available when I needed information or advice. William David Barry, of the MHS Research Library and the author of many books, and Herb Adams, a good friend and writer of numerous historical newspaper and magazine pieces, generously shared their knowledge and counsel.

Of great help with the visual aspect of the book was Kathy Amoroso, Director of Digital Projects at MHS. She acted as my road map to finding the photos and illustrations that make up such a large portion of this work.

Webster Bull of Commonwealth Editions and I had a chance meeting one Saturday afternoon early in 2006, and from that conversation came the writing of this book. I will always be grateful for our meeting and his faith.

Finally, I want to dedicate *A Short History of Portland* to my first and (thus far) only grandson, Vaughn Grenier Levinsky, born at the beginning of the project, in the hope that it will be helpful in his understanding of the history of the city of his birth.

# index

# illustration credits

From the Collections of the Maine Historical Society:
Pages 2, 3, 6, 7, 13, 15, 16, 17, 19, 20, 26, 28, 29 (both), 30, 32, 35, 36, 39, 40, 45, 46 (both), 47, 48, 49 (both), 53, 54, 55, 59, 60, 61 (bottom), 63, 64, 66 (all), 67 (bottom), 68, 69, 70 (bottom), 71, 73, 74, 77, 79, 80, 82 (both), 83, 84, 86 (all), 87, 88, 89 (both), 90 (both), 92 (both), 93, 94, 95 (both), 96 (both), 97, 98, 99, 101, 103 (top), 104 (both), 107, 109 (both), 110 (top two), 111 (bottom)

From the Collections of the Maine Historical Society and the Maine State Museum:
Page 61 (top)

From the Collections of the Maine Historical Society, copyright Blethen Maine Newspapers:
Page 75

Courtesy of George J. Mitchell Department of Special Collections and Archives, Bowdoin College Library, Brunswick, Maine:
Page 50

Courtesy of Portland Public Library:
Page 67 (top)

Courtesy of Portland Harbor Museum/Angell Collection:
Page 70 (top)

From www.gordonsofmaine.com:
Page 78

From the Collections of W. & C. Barry, Portland, Maine:
Page 81

Courtesy of Friends of the Kotzschmar Organ:
Page 91

Courtesy of Libra Foundation, photo by Tom Jones:
Page 102

Courtesy of Portland Sea Dogs:
Page 103 (bottom)

Courtesy of Judd Nelson:
Page 105

Courtesy of Maine Medical Center:
Page 110 (bottom)

Photos by the author:
Pages 11, 58, 106, 111 (top)